Rebuilding
For Divorce and Beyond

The Divorce Helpbook for Kids

Cynthia MacGregor

Impact Publishers®
ATASCADERO, CALIFORNIA

ATTENTION ORGANIZATIONS AND CORPORATIONS:
This book is available at quantity discounts on bulk purchases for educational, business, or sales promotional use. For further information, please contact Impact Publishers, P.O. Box 6016, Atascadero, CA 93423-6016. Phone: 1-800-246-7228, e-mail: sales@impactpublishers.com

Library of Congress Cataloging-in-Publication Data

MacGregor, Cynthia.
    The divorce helpbook for kids / Cynthia MacGregor.
      p. cm. — (Rebuilding books, for divorce and beyond)
    Includes bibliographical references and index.
    Summary: A guide to dealing with the divorce of parents, discussing various reasons for divorce, the emotions experienced by the children, and ways of coping with the change.
    ISBN 1-886230-39-0 (alk. paper)
    1. Children of divorced parents—Juvenile literature. 2. Divorce—Juvenile. literature. 3. Broken homes—Juvenile literature. [1. Divorce.] I. Title. II. Series.

HQ777.5 .M33 2001
306.89—dc21

                                          2001024974

Publisher's Note
This publication is designed to provide accurate and authoritative information in regard to the subject matter covered. It is sold with the understanding that the publisher is not engaged in rendering psychological, legal, or other professional services. If expert assistance or counseling is needed, the services of a competent professional should be sought.

Impact Publishers and colophon are registered trademarks of Impact Publishers, Inc.

Cover design by Sharon Wood-Schnare and Kathy Richardson, San Luis Obispo, California
Printed in the United States of America on recycled, acid-free paper.
Published by ***Impact ♲ Publishers*** ®
POST OFFICE BOX 6016
ATASCADERO, CALIFORNIA 93423-6016
www.impactpublishers.com

*This book is for all kids
who have to go through
their parents getting divorced.
My daughter went through it
when her father and I got divorced.
It was rough on her.
I hope this book helps a little
to make it easier for you.*

CONTENTS

1

"Things Are Different at Home Now"

Paige had a terrible day at school. She got a "C" on a test in math — her best and favorite subject. She got into a fight with her best friend, Hannah. One of the other girls dropped her tray in the cafeteria and got meat loaf gravy all over Paige. It was an accident, but still Paige had to "wear" a gravy stain on her shirt all day.

At 3:30, Paige got home from school. At last! Just opening the front door made her feel better. As she walked into her house, she could smell something delicious cooking in the kitchen.

As she passed through the living room, she saw the family portrait. It had been hanging on the wall for years. It showed her mom and dad, her older brother (as he had looked five years ago), and Paige herself. (Of course, she had been a really little kid at the time.)

From upstairs, she heard her brother practicing on his saxophone. Barry hit a sour note, and Paige winced. But even as she cringed at her brother's musical mistake, Paige began to relax.

It had been a bad day, but she was home now. Home to the familiar sights and smells and sounds. Home, where things were comfortable and familiar. Home, where she felt safe and protected.

◆ ◆ ◆

Ryan's day at school had been pretty good. This week, Mrs. Hilton's class was studying dinosaurs, which interested him a lot. He got a "B+" on a difficult project he'd worked hard on, and he was pleased with the grade. And the school lunch had been meatballs and spaghetti — his favorite.

On the bus coming home, one of the boys started singing a song that had been playing a lot on the radio. Ryan started goofing around with the song, singing different words to it. He made up his own words to the song's tune.

The first verse of Ryan's version was all about mean teachers and tough tests. The second verse was about the food in the school cafeteria. (The meatballs and spaghetti were good, but some of the lunches were super-gross!)

The kids who were sitting near Ryan laughed a lot at his made-up verses to the song. "That's pretty funny!" one boy said. Another asked him if he planned to write songs when he grew up. "I'll bet you could win a Grammy Award!" he said. And a bunch of kids applauded him.

Ryan felt really good when he got off the bus. But as he walked up the street to his house, his good mood started to wear off. The closer he got to home, the worse he felt. Soon he started walking slower, making it take longer till he got in the front door.

When he opened the front door, everything looked the same as always. But then he walked into the living room, looking for his mother.

Once again he saw the almost-square place on the carpet where the color was brighter, less faded. It was the place where his dad's recliner used to be. Next he saw the empty place over the mantel where the picture of his grandparents — his dad's parents — had hung. Other pictures were gone, too.

The end table next to where his dad's chair had been looked different, too. It was neat and clean . . . and empty. And depressing.

Ryan had come home, but he had left his good mood outside the front door. It hadn't come

*home with him. Ryan didn't want to feel out of
sorts and unhappy. But lately, he couldn't feel
happy at home anymore.*

*Not since his dad had moved out. Things sure
are different at home now.*

When you were younger, and you hurt yourself, or
some other kid bullied you, wasn't it always a comfort
to know you could go home? Home . . . where
everything was comfortable and familiar and safe.

Home. No matter what happened to you on the
outside, home was still home. The neighbors might get
mad at you if you trampled their flowers while chasing
a ball. Your friends might not play fair. You could fall
off your bike or lose your favorite toy, but you always
felt safe when you got home. Home... the one place
where nothing changed and you always felt secure.

But maybe that's no longer true for you. If your
parents have recently gotten a divorce, or are in the
process of getting one, it's probably made a big
difference in your home life.

What are some of the changes you've noticed?

• The biggest change is probably that one of your
parents — most likely your dad — has moved out of
the house. And you probably miss him a lot! (Or you
miss your mom, if she's the one who moved out.)

• Along with your dad or mom being gone, his or her

clothes, other belongings, and maybe even some furniture is probably gone from your house too.

• It's possible that your parents tell you, "We can't afford that," or "That's too expensive for us," more often than they used to.

• You might have moved to a new house or apartment, and maybe even changed schools.

• If your mom didn't used to work, maybe she's gone back to work since your parents split up.

• If your mom used to work part-time, she might now be working full-time instead.

• Dinnertime (and other family meals) probably feels kind of lonely without Dad or Mom sitting at the table in his or her usual spot.

• You've probably been given extra chores or responsibilities around the house.

How do all these changes make you feel? Probably pretty sad a lot of the time. Maybe you get an "empty" or achy feeling inside. Here are some of the things we're going to talk about in this book:

• Reasons why some parents get divorced.

• Some of the ways your life might change if your parents divorce.

• How you probably feel about the divorce.

• Things you can do that will help you feel better.

• Who you can go to, to talk about the bad feelings you may have inside you because of the divorce.

• What's likely to happen in your house in the months ahead.

I'll try to answer as many of your questions as I can — including, possibly, some you haven't even thought of yet.

I Know What Divorce Feels Like

Do you wonder who I am to talk about divorce like this? Well, I'm a writer with over thirty published books, but even more than that, I'm a divorced mom. Yup . . . I did to my daughter exactly what your parents have done to you.

It wasn't easy.

It wasn't easy for her. It wasn't easy for me.

Believe me . . . no parent wants to make his or her kids feel bad.

It probably seems to you that your parents are thinking only of themselves. If they wanted to make you feel good, they wouldn't have broken up their marriage. That's not true. It wasn't true for me. It probably isn't true for your parents either.

But when you're fighting a lot — or just not talking to each other — things aren't happy around the house. And it rubs off on your kids. It doesn't make for a happy situation. The way things were going in my marriage didn't make things happy for my daughter. And if your parents had stayed married, it wouldn't have made things happy for you either.

But I helped my daughter get through living with divorced parents.

And I want to help you, too!

I want to help you because I've been there. I've seen what effects divorce can have on a child. I've seen what it did to my daughter. And I've seen that it's not the end of the world. I've seen that she could cope. She could get past it. She could live with the effects of divorce.

And you can too.

Not only that, but I've been through it *again* — with my grandkids. Yes, my daughter is now grown up and divorced herself. Now her own kids are dealing with the same heavy stuff she went through when she was a kid. But she can help them get through it a little more easily, because she's done it herself. "Been there, done that," as the saying goes.

Now, I don't want anyone to get the wrong idea: Yes, I got divorced, and my daughter also got divorced, but the two divorces are not related. If you come from a divorced family, that does not mean that when you grow up, you're likely to get divorced yourself!

But because my daughter knows what it's like to have divorced parents, it's been easier for her to understand what her own kids are going through because of her divorce. So an unfortunate thing (she had to deal with her own parents' divorce when she was a kid) has turned out to have a good side to it (she is able to help her own kids and understand what they're going through).

And watching my grandkids cope with living in a divorced family has helped me write this book, just like watching my daughter cope with my own divorce helped me write it.

My daughter got through it. My grandkids are getting through it.

You can get through it too.

I know it doesn't seem easy. I didn't say it would be easy. It isn't. But *you can do it.*

And this book will help.

Ready? Let's get going.

A Note to Readers:

• Divorce is different for each family that goes through it. You may live with your mom or your dad, or go back and forth between them. So, sometimes I'll be writing about your *dad* saying or doing something when for you it's your *mom* that says or does it — as you read, you can change it to the right parent for you.

• You may want to keep a journal nearby as you read, so that you can write down any thoughts and feelings that you may want to remember later.

• If you find a chapter confusing or hard to understand, you may want to ask your dad or mom to read it with you so that you can talk together about any questions you may have.

2

"Why Can't My Parents Stay Married?"

The first question you probably have is:

Why does everything have to change? I liked it better when my parents were married and everyone lived together.

You liked it better for two reasons. One reason is that it's nice to have both your parents living in the same house with you, to have your family together. The other reason is that we are always most comfortable with what's *familiar*.

When you were really little, you probably had a favorite blanket, a favorite toy, and other familiar things that you especially liked. When you were sad, when you got hurt, when your parents were angry with you, or when it thundered and you were scared, these familiar objects were a comfort to you. You could hold onto your toy, or your blanket, and feel safer.

Even now, you probably get comfort from familiar things. Maybe you have a favorite shirt. When you wear it, you feel good. You might still have a favorite toy (though a different one than your favorite from years ago). When you play with it, you feel safe and comforted. You might have a CD or tape that helps you feel good when you play it.

If you have a pet, playing with him or her probably makes you feel better. And spending time with your best friend is good, too. You know and like your friend and can trust him or her.

Later on, we'll talk about how these things can help you feel better when you feel upset about your parents' divorce. Right now, though, I've mentioned them for a different reason:

Those things — the toy, your old blanket, your favorite song, your pet, and your friend, as well as other favorite things that have been around awhile — make you feel good for several different reasons. One of them is that they are so *familiar*. New things are exciting. It's fun to get new toys, read new books, make new friends. Changes can be exciting, too. But even happy changes can sometimes leave you feeling anxious. Have you ever changed schools? Maybe your new school was better. Maybe the kids were nicer. Maybe you liked your new teacher better. But I'll bet you had "butterflies in your stomach" on the first day at the new school . . . and maybe for a lot more days than that. You missed your old school that you were used to, because what's familiar is always more comfortable. Almost everyone feels most comfortable when they're with familiar things, in a familiar place, with familiar people. And almost everyone feels more comfortable when things in their lives stay the same.

Why am I talking about new schools and old toys? Because I want you to be aware of how comforting familiar things and familiar ways of doing things are. I want you to understand that one of the other reasons a divorce can be upsetting is the change in routine that goes with it.

Not only do you miss your dad or mom a lot, now that he or she no longer lives with you, but you miss the comfortable feeling of how things used to be. Change is unsettling. And many changes go along with a divorce.

What Are Some Possible Changes?

• Your parents don't both live with you anymore.

• If your dad used to drive you to school before, it might be your mom now, you might take the bus, or ride with a carpool, or some other arrangement.

• If you've moved, you might be going to a different school now and having to make new friends.

• Dinner might be served earlier or later than before, or eaten in the kitchen instead of the dining room.

• Your mom might cook different foods now, things your dad didn't like to eat. Or maybe you eat out more often because your mom or dad works more and doesn't have as much time to prepare meals.

• If it's your mom who moved out, your dad might not cook all the same things your mom did. He might not cook as well. Or he might just cook *differently*. Maybe you are learning how to cook now, so that you can be of more help to your mom or dad.

• You might be left alone in the house more often. Or left alone for the first time. That might make you feel more grown-up, or maybe even at times a little scared.

Because change is upsetting to so many people, some kids are as upset by the changes in their routine as they are by the fact that Dad (or Mom) no longer lives with them.

Why Did My Parents Have to Stop Being Married? Why Couldn't Things Have Gone on the Way They Were?

There are lots of reasons why people get divorced. But most of the different reasons come down to one of two things:

• They don't love each other any more.

• They still love each other, but they just can't get along.

Will They Stop Loving Me, Too?

You might fear that: *If they don't love each other, maybe they'll stop loving me, too!*

Impossible!

The kind of love a parent feels for a child is a very special kind of love. No matter how upset they get with you, how annoyed they get with you, how angry they get with you, how disappointed they get in you, parents who love you *will not* stop loving you.

They may yell, or look sad, or get stern, lecture you, or even seem like they're not paying much attention to you, but they will still love you.

They may not like something you did. They may not like your attitude this evening. They may not like the way you behaved last night. They may not like the way you talked to your sister or brother. *But they still love you, and that will never stop.*

The love parents feel for their children is something like the love children feel for their parents. Sometimes you get very angry at your mom or dad. Sometimes you're steaming mad at something they've said, or something they won't let you do. But you get over it. And you always still love them . . . no matter what they say or do, no matter how angry you get at them. Right?

It's the same with the love parents have for their kids. It's a very special kind of love. No matter how angry they get at you, *that doesn't mean they don't love you.*

Even if they stop loving each other, they will never stop loving you.

You may be thinking, *"But Dad's been yelling at me a lot lately. I don't think he likes anything I do anymore."*

It probably isn't you. You *might* have been doing more things that get on your dad's nerves; after all, you're having a hard time now, too. But the chances are he's just not very happy, and you're catching some of the flak.

You know how you feel when you fail a test in school *and* the school lunch is fish cakes *and* you accidentally tear your favorite jeans *and* you get in a fight on the way home? You're so unhappy you might even snap at your best friend or snarl at your mom or ignore your dog. Right?

Well, your parents try not to take it out on you when they're not feeling happy. But they're human, too. When things are really unpleasant for them, they get in bad moods . . . just like you do. They get short-tempered. They get annoyed more easily. Things you do that normally wouldn't bother them very much irritate them more. Your parents become impatient or cross with you. You wind up getting snapped at or snarled at — and that can really hurt.

How Did All This Happen to My Mom & Dad?

It isn't easy for parents to divorce. What comes before the divorce isn't very easy, either.

➤ *What do you mean? What comes before the divorce?*

What comes before the divorce is the reason for the divorce. In fact, there are lots of possible reasons. But think about the two most common reasons: they don't love each other anymore, or they still love each other, but they can't get along.

If your mom and dad can't get along anymore, they've probably been fighting a lot. You might have heard them. (Or they might wait to argue till you're not listening. You might not have had any idea that there was a problem between them.) It's no fun to live with someone you fight with all the time. Would you like to live like that?

So maybe your dad and mom have been arguing a lot lately. Or maybe they've been talking about the possibility of getting a divorce. It hasn't been a very happy time for them.

➤ *But I fight with my friends, and the next day we're friends again. Why can't Mom and Dad make up with each other like we do?*

It's not that easy. Maybe they had lots of fights, made up each time, and then got into more fights. They don't want to keep on fighting all the time. Even if you make up each time, it's not good to keep on fighting.

And their fights are probably more serious than your fights with your friends. The things two parents — or, a married couple — fight about are usually different from the kinds of things two kids who are friends fight about.

If they stay married but can't get along, that's not fair to you, either. If your parents fight a lot, or stop talking to each other, they won't be in good moods. They'll probably snap at you, or be annoyed by little things you do — things they used to be able to ignore.

➢ *But I never hear my parents fighting.*

They may fight only when you're not listening. Or they may not be fighting the way you and your friends fight. There are lots of different ways people act with each other when they're not getting along. Out-and-out arguing, fighting, and name-calling aren't the only ways people can behave with each other when they don't get along. They might avoid each other, ignore each other, or just pretend that nothing is wrong.

Always Remember: It's Not Your Fault!

➢*If I make my bed every morning, study hard and get all "A"s in school, and don't play the radio too loud, do you think Daddy might stay?*

Now, pay close attention. This is very important: *Your parents are not breaking up with each other because of anything you did! It's not your fault!*

It's easy to blame yourself when things go wrong around you. And if your parents have been more easily annoyed with you lately, because they're unhappy, you could easily get confused. You could think that Dad (or Mom) is leaving because he or she is so unhappy with you these days. *But that's simply not true!*

This is so important that I'm going to say it again — in capital letters: IT'S NOT YOUR FAULT! It is not your responsibility that they are getting a divorce.

◆ ◆ ◆

Corey's parents hadn't been getting along for a while. They snapped at each other. There was a lot of tension in the house. Dinnertime was no fun.

They didn't get along with Corey, either. Though he tried not to be mean to his little brother, and tried to do all his chores, nothing he did seemed to please them, especially his father.

One day, Corey's dad told Corey that very soon he would be moving to an apartment nearby. He said he would spend a lot of time with Corey, and that Corey could spend some weekends at his apartment, but Corey didn't want his dad to move out.

Corey's dad had been complaining a lot lately about Corey not doing his chores on time. Corey started doing all his chores without fail. He even started doing extra things to help around the house.

Another thing Corey and his dad had argued about was Corey's homework. He started doing his homework as soon as he got home from school. Corey also started being extra-nice to his little brother. And he even ate cauliflower whenever his mom cooked it!

Whatever Corey's dad had complained about, Corey changed. He even improved himself in ways his dad had never mentioned. Yet in two weeks, his dad moved out.

Corey was crushed. "But you yelled at me about all these things, and I changed them. I'm doing my homework. I'm doing my chores. I've changed everything you ever complained about. Why are you moving anyhow?" Corey asked.

Corey felt his father had cheated him. What Corey didn't understand was that his father wasn't moving because of anything Corey had done (or hadn't done). Corey's dad and mom weren't getting along. They were both unhappy, especially Corey's dad.

Because Corey's dad was unhappy, it was easier for him to be unhappy about *everything*. Anything that had bothered him before bothered him even more now. And if Corey didn't do his homework or his chores, his dad had more to say about it than he used to.

But the main thing that was making his dad unhappy had nothing to do with Corey. Corey's dad wasn't moving out because of Corey. And though Corey's parents were glad about him changing his behavior, it didn't make any difference.

The reason for the divorce had nothing to do with Corey, and nothing that Corey did could change the fact that his parents weren't going to stay married. The same is true for you: your parents are not getting divorced because of you. And nothing you say or do can make them stay together.

You are not to blame. You are not at fault.

And you cannot "fix" things between them, either.

If It's Not My Fault, Whose Fault Is It?

Not every situation is that simple. You can't always blame someone. It's very likely that neither your mom nor your dad did anything on purpose to each other to make each other unhappy. It's certain that they didn't give up and decide to get divorced after just one fight.

There are many different reasons why people get divorced. The *reason* in your parents' case *doesn't really matter. It doesn't change anything.* Whatever the reason, you can be sure your parents think it's a good one. And you can be sure they tried to work their problems out before they finally agreed to get a divorce.

Here's what you need to know:

• They didn't decide to get a divorce after just one fight.

• They didn't decide to get a divorce just to hurt you. That's the last thing they want to do.

• They didn't decide to get divorced just to be mean, either to you or to each other.

• They didn't decide to get a divorce because of something you did, or didn't do.

• They're unhappy being married to each other.

• If they're unhappy with each other, they're going to be unhappy with a lot of things. As a result, you're likely to be less happy, too.

• As hard as it may be to believe this, things will get better.

Why Can't My Parents Get Along?

➤ *They're always telling my friends and me that we have to learn to get along. Why doesn't that go for them, too?*

It isn't that simple. I wish it were. (I'll bet you wish it were, too!)

Sometimes people change. They may change in ways that make them better. They may change in ways that aren't better or worse, just *different*. Or they may change in ways that other people find harder to deal with. And trying harder to get along just isn't the answer.

Another problem is that sometimes people develop different interests after a while. For instance, when your parents got married, maybe they both liked to go bowling together, or do the crossword puzzle together, or play cards with each other, or work side-by-side in the garden. And now they may not enjoy doing those things.

Maybe your mom no longer finds bowling to be fun, or your dad no longer wants to play cards. Perhaps instead your dad likes to fix up old cars, or go bird-watching, and your mom doesn't care to do these things. Perhaps your mom has learned to play golf or likes to go on hikes, but your dad doesn't want to do those things with her.

You've probably had something similar happen to you. You might have had a friend you liked to spend time with. At first you enjoyed the same activities. But later, your interests grew different.

◆ ◆ ◆

Scott and Mike were good friends. They both liked to skate together, and they always had a good time.

Then Scott's parents got a computer, and Scott started spending a lot of time with it. He played computer games, made up stories and typed them up, and explored the kids' "chat room" of an online service.

Meanwhile, Mike got a stamp collection from his grandma for Christmas. Suddenly, Mike started spending a lot of time with that stamp collection. He spent hours putting stamps in albums, trading stamps with other kids, visiting stores that sell stamps to collectors, and reading stamp collectors' magazines.

Mike made some new friends, too: kids who also had stamp collections and could trade stamps with him.

Mike tried to talk to Scott about his stamp collection. Scott wasn't really interested, but because it was important to Mike, he listened.

After a little while, though, Scott got bored. He tried to change the subject to computers. Computers interested him a lot. But Mike wasn't interested in computers at all, and he tried to change the subject back to stamps.

This happened often. Neither Mike nor Scott wanted to go skating anymore. Mike's big interest was stamps, but Scott didn't care about them. He didn't have a collection, so he couldn't trade stamps with Mike. He didn't know what Mike was talking about when he talked about "mint stamps" and "first-day issues" and "commemoratives."

And when Scott talked about "chat rooms" and "smileys" and "e-mail," Mike didn't know what Scott was talking about. Mike didn't care, either. He didn't have a computer. He didn't especially want to have a computer. And he didn't want to talk to Scott about computers.

Mike and Scott found that they no longer had much in common. They didn't have anything to talk about. And they didn't enjoy being with each other that much anymore.

Pretty soon, they stopped spending so much time together. Mike and Scott had both grown to have different interests. Mike didn't want to do what Scott enjoyed. He didn't even like talking about it. And Scott didn't enjoy Mike's hobby or want to talk about it either.

Eventually they weren't friends anymore. It's not that they became enemies or anything like that. They just no longer enjoyed each other's company.

Something similar can happen to grown-ups who are married. If they develop different interests, and they don't share those interests, they can wind up having nothing fun to do together. They can wind up with very little to talk about. They can wind up not enjoying spending time together.

They might try to find some activities or hobbies they can share. But maybe they really just don't enjoy doing things together anymore. Maybe the things each of them likes to talk about don't interest each other anymore.

This isn't anyone's fault! Nobody did anything wrong. Nobody was being mean. Nobody should "stop it." Nobody is to blame.

3

"What's Going to Happen Now?"

The next thing you need to know is: whether your parents are married or divorced, you're all still a family. If your mom and dad are divorced, they're no longer each other's husband and wife, but they are still — and they always will be — your mom and dad.

Your living arrangements will change, and other things will change too, but your mom is still your mom, and your dad is still your dad. The relatives on both sides of the family are all still your relatives.

➤ *But who's going to live where?*

That's a very good question! Years ago, when two parents divorced, the judge almost always granted custody to the mother.

➤ *Custody? What's that?*

Well, here's an example: if your mom has custody of you, that means you live with her. It means she's the one who mostly gets to say whether you're going to spend the summer at home or at camp or at some relative's house. She decides if you get to spend the night at a friend's house, go to the skate park, or wear that outfit in public. She usually makes you do your homework or tells you if you can watch TV. It means she makes most of the decisions about you.

But these days, the mother doesn't automatically get custody anymore. Sometimes the judge will make a different decision:

• The judge might give custody of the kids to the father instead.

• If the parents have both a son and a daughter, the judge might give custody of the girl to the mom and custody of the boy to the father.

• The judge might award what's called "joint custody" or "shared custody." That means your mom and dad each have an equal say in decisions about you, and you probably live part of the time with each of them. Maybe you'll stay half the week with your mom and half the week with your dad. Or maybe one week you'll live at your mom's house, and the next week you'll live at your dad's house.

• Sometimes a judge will even listen to what a child has to say. It depends on the judge and also on how old you are, but some judges will at least listen to what some kids want. That doesn't mean you automatically get your wish. You may tell the judge you want to live with your dad, but the judge decides it's best for you to live with your mom anyhow. But you *might* get a chance to express an opinion.

➤ *If I live with my mom, will I ever see my dad again?*

Of course! You'll probably see your dad a lot! Normally, when one parent gets custody, the other one gets "visitation rights." You might get to visit with your dad every other weekend for the whole weekend, or every Sunday, and maybe some time during the week, too. (Or, of course, if you live with your dad, it's your mom you'll be visiting on weekends, or whatever arrangement your parents and the judge work out.) Sometimes the parent you don't live with might have to move to a different city for his or her job. It can make it a little harder to see that parent as often as you see your "custodial" parent. But when that happens, it usually just means that you'll spend more holidays, vacations and other times when you're out of school with the parent you don't live with.

➤ *Why is there a judge? Did one of my parents do something bad?*

Not all judges and courts are for trials. Not everyone who goes to court is accused of committing a crime. There are other reasons why people go to court. And one of those reasons is to get divorced.

Your parents have to divide up all the things they own. And they have to work out details about money. And — perhaps most important of all — they have to work out the details that involve you. Like who you're going to live with, and when your other parent will get to see you. Some judges do nothing all day but listen to people who are getting divorced and help them settle the details of the divorce.

➤ *Who gets to keep the house where we're living now — Mom or Dad?*

There's no one set answer to that question. It depends on many things.

• Most often the kids get to live with their mom. And the mom gets to keep the house. But it doesn't always work like that.

• Sometimes the dad gets the kids and the house.

• Sometimes it's too expensive to keep up payments on the house *and* pay for the other parent to live somewhere else, so both parents move.

• Sometimes a mom who used to stay home during the day goes back to work after a divorce. And sometimes she wants to move across town, or to the next town, to be nearer to the job she's taken. (Sometimes the dad needs to move for his job, too.)

• Sometimes a mom and her kids move out to live with another relative, who can help the mom take care of the kids. Or she might move in with another mom who's also divorced and has kids living with her. The two can share the responsibility of watching the kids. They also can take turns with the cooking, house cleaning, shopping, and other chores.

• Sometimes both the mom and dad move out because they want to start over in a new house. It feels like they're getting a fresh start if they move to a whole new house.

➤ *If I live with my mom, when do I get to see my dad? (Or if I live with my dad, when do I get to see my mom?)*

That depends mostly on the visitation agreement that gets worked out at the time of your parents' divorce. If you live with your mom, your dad will have regular visitation rights. He might see you every Sunday, or every other weekend. He might get to see you on one weeknight, too. Or maybe he'll get you for two weeks over the summer.

➤ *What if Dad moves out of town — or my mom and I do?*

Then you won't get to see him as often, but you *will* get to see him! Probably you'll spend at least some school vacations with him. You might also spend a larger chunk of your summer vacation with him than you would if he lived nearby.

➤ *Wow — it sounds like there are going to be a lot of changes in my life! What else is going to change?*

• Besides some moving and changes in living arrangements, the main change is likely to be that your mom may have to go to work (if she's not already working).

• Another change that you're likely to notice is that your mom and dad may have less money than before. Certainly they'll see to it that you have food and clothes and everything that's necessary. But you may not be able to get as many new clothes as before. You may not be able to go to the movies as often. They may tell you that you have to eat less take-out in order to save money.

• On the other hand, your mom may have less time to cook, and you may wind up eating more take-out, instead of less!

• If you're old enough, you may even be asked to help with the cooking. You will almost certainly have more chores around the house, too. If you never had to do the dishes before, you may be asked to do them now. Possibly you'll be asked to do the laundry sometimes, or to take out the garbage. What chores you'll have to do will depend on several things. These include your age and whether you have any brothers or sisters to share the chores.

• If your mom works full-time, you may be alone at home when you come home from school in the afternoons. Or your parents may make arrangements for you to go to a neighbor's after school, or to an after-school program at your school. Or maybe there will be someone else to take care of you at your house when you get home.

• Your parents may seem sad sometimes. Even when parents both agree that divorce is the best thing for them, they aren't always happy about it.

You've probably made decisions that you knew were best for you but that didn't always leave you completely happy. Maybe you adopted a big dog even though your house doesn't have a big yard. You may have realized the dog wasn't happy without room to run around in. The dog may even have chewed up your toys and clothes and papers because it was unhappy. If that's ever happened to you, you probably had to give the dog away to someone with lots of room for the dog to run. You knew you'd made the best decision, but you weren't happy about it. In a way, divorces can be like that.

4

Dealing with Feelings

When parents get divorced, their kids go through a wide range of feelings . . . or bottle themselves up and feel nothing. Some kids just "shut down." Instead of feeling all the hurt and anger that most kids feel, they turn off their feelings and don't feel anything at all. It's not just the divorce that they don't feel anything about. Their feelings about other things get turned off like a faucet, too.

◆ ◆ ◆

Evan's parents got divorced right before Christmas. Evan thought he'd feel really upset, but instead, he hardly felt anything at all. Unfortunately, that was true about everything in Evan's life. Not only didn't he feel really sad about the divorce, he didn't feel much excitement about Christmas that year, either.

It was two weeks before Christmas, and the stores were full of decorations, but he hardly noticed. Some of his favorite Christmas specials were on TV, but when Evan's mom said, "Charlie Brown and Snoopy are on tonight," Evan said, "I don't care."

The last week of school before vacation, there was a very tough math test. Evan got a 100% on the test. He got all the answers right! The teacher was so proud of him, she praised him in front of the whole class. Evan didn't care.

The last day of school, all the other kids cheered when the bell rang and class was over, but Evan didn't feel excited about vacation.

Evan got lots of really great Christmas presents. He even got the new bike he'd been begging his dad for. But he hardly cared — it just didn't seem to matter.

Kids like Evan don't turn off their emotions on purpose. They don't choose to stop feeling anything. That's just the way some people protect themselves from too much hurt.

If they have a birthday, or their favorite relatives come to visit, they don't feel happy. If their best friends move out of town, they don't feel sad. If teachers unfairly accuse them of starting trouble in school, or cheating, or passing notes, they don't feel angry. They just don't feel. They don't feel anything at all.

Most kids do feel a wild jumble of emotions during a divorce and for a while afterward. The two strongest emotions are **anger** and **sadness**.

And, it's normal to feel all those feelings — or to feel nothing at all. But just because it's normal, that doesn't mean it's good. You want to get over feeling such strong emotions — or feeling nothing at all — because it's not a healthy or happy way to live. The good news is that there are some different things you can do to help yourself.

What's Happening with Your Emotions?

Anger. Sometimes, instead of acting mad at the person you're really angry at — in this case, your parents — you take it out on someone else instead.

Maybe you get in fights with your friends. You don't know why, but suddenly you feel mad at them all the time. You get angry at the littlest things. You think your friends are being mean, or unfair, or disloyal.

Suddenly, your favorite teacher is getting on your nerves, too. Why does she call on you all the time? Or why doesn't he call on you when you know the answer? The whole world is unfair:

➤ *The school lunches are worse than ever. Yuk!*

➤ *My stupid dog poops ten times more than she used to, and I have to clean it up. Gross!*

➤ *The crossing guard lets traffic start coming again just before I get to the corner. She's so mean!*

➤ *I can't find the new issue of my favorite comic book at any dumb store. It's not fair!*

➤ *The whole world is against me! The whole world hates me! I hate the whole world!*

No, you don't. You're just very angry. But being angry at your friends, your teachers, and other people who have nothing to do with what's upsetting you really doesn't do any good. After all, they really haven't done anything to you. It's your parents' divorce that you're really upset about.

On the other hand, being angry at your parents doesn't help, either. Sure, it's understandable that you would be. You don't have both your parents living with you anymore. They've changed your home, your whole life.

But they didn't do this to *you*. I mean, *they didn't do it to try to hurt you*. In fact, they probably thought twice and then twice again about getting divorced, just because of you. If they wound up getting divorced, *in spite of how it hurt you*, then they must have thought it really was necessary for them to do.

Go ahead . . . be angry. But don't be angry at them.

In a minute, we'll talk about ways to help yourself feel better.

Sadness. Instead of, or along with, anger, you may be feeling a great deal of sadness. You may just feel "down" all the time. When good things happen, you don't feel happy about them. Maybe you even cry a lot.

That's OK. It's OK whether you're a girl or a boy. Go ahead and cry. It helps get the bad feelings out. In fact, it's one thing you can do that will help you feel better in the long run.

Don't make yourself cry if you don't feel like it. But if you do feel like it, go ahead and let the tears out. (If you're in the middle of school, you might try to wait till you can have some privacy, like in the restroom, or till you go home. Or ask your teacher if it would be OK to step outside the classroom when you feel you need to.)

You Can Help Yourself Feel Better

• **Hit a pillow.** Punch a soft pillow with your fist, or thump it really hard with a tennis racket. If you don't have a tennis racket, use something else that won't get ruined by hitting the pillow and that won't ruin the pillow either. (For instance, don't use anything sharp. Don't use anything too large or really heavy. If you lose your grip on it, you could hurt yourself or something else.)

• **Yell.** Pick a time when nobody's at home (or warn whoever is home that you'll be making some noise). Close the windows so the neighbors won't hear you, and you can even stand in a closet, or get under your blanket. Then yell all the angry words you need to let out. Yell at the world. You can even yell at your parents. Let it all out from inside you. If you feel like crying, or screaming some more, or stamping your feet, do it. You'll feel better afterward.

• **Pour your feelings out on paper.** Write down everything you feel. This isn't a composition for school. It doesn't have to be in logical order, with topic sentences and proper punctuation and all that other stuff teachers tell you to do. Your grammar doesn't have to be good. Your spelling doesn't count. Neither does your handwriting. Just write what you feel. Let it flow out.

If you want, you can think of this as a letter to yourself. Or think of it as a letter to your mom or dad, *a letter they're never going to see.* If you feel angry at them for getting divorced, here's the place to say so. Let the feelings pour out of you. Say anything you want. Then tear the paper up in little pieces afterward. Nobody has to know what you wrote. In fact, it's better if you keep it to yourself. It's really just for you.

It doesn't have to be a letter, though. It doesn't have to be anything. It doesn't even have to make sense. Just write what you feel.

• **Cuddle your favorite toy.** Maybe, just for a little while, you want to sleep with your old teddy bear again. Do you have an old shirt or sweater that always felt snuggly and cozy? Wear it. Maybe it no longer fits well enough for you to wear it to school. Maybe it has too many holes for you to even wear it to play outside the house. But you can still wear it around the house. You can even wear it to bed.

If your mom or dad says anything about it, just tell him or her that wearing it makes you feel better. You can even remind your parents, "This isn't an easy time for me. Wearing this shirt helps me feel better."

• **Listen to your favorite tape or CD . . . maybe an old favorite, from when you were younger.** Music has a strong power over our feelings. It can touch us deep inside. It can soothe us. It can help us feel better.

• **Watch a sad movie.** If you feel like you need to cry, but you can't quite get the tears out, watch a movie that makes you cry. If you have a videotape of a movie that has that effect on you, great. If not, ask your mom or dad to rent one for you.

You don't have to explain why, if you don't want to. You can just say that you want to see it. If anyone asks you why, simply say that the movie will help you feel better.

• **Write a story about a kid whose parents get divorced.** Make up a story. Try to write a realistic happy ending. Sure, you could write that the kid's parents got back together, but that isn't very realistic. It happens once in a while, but not in most cases. Almost every child wants it to turn out that way, but it hardly every does in real life.

Wouldn't it be better to write about how the child learned to deal with the parents being divorced? Then you can try to make your real life like that of the child in the story.

But if, right now, you don't feel like writing a happy ending, that's OK, too. Write what you feel. Write what makes you feel better. Sometimes you have to first feel sad before you can feel happy again. And sometimes you have to write sad stories.

• **Draw pictures.** For some kids, art is very helpful when they feel bad. Draw pictures of whatever you want. (Of course, you don't have to just draw — you might prefer to paint, instead.)

• **Put on a puppet show.** You can write a script for the show, or you can just make up the words as you go along.

You probably want to have the puppets talk to each other about divorce, since that's what's on your mind. But if you feel as if your mother or father has deserted you by moving out, you can always put on a puppet show about somebody being deserted.

If you feel as if your parents are being unfair to you

by getting divorced, you can put on a puppet show about somebody being unfair to someone else.

You can let the puppets act out your own situation, or another situation that reminds you of it. Let the puppets talk for you, if you want. It's your show.

• **Keep a diary or journal.** Your diary is for your eyes only. You can pour your deepest feelings into it every day, knowing nobody else is going to see it. Of course, you'll want to keep it in a safe place.

Confide in your diary or journal. Tell it your feelings, your secrets, your wishes, your disappointments. Tell it anything or everything.

Diaries and journals aren't for girls only. Some of the famous men who have kept diaries or journals include the famous American writers Mark Twain, Nathaniel Hawthorne, and Henry David Thoreau.

• **Help other kids . . . and help yourself . . . by writing a play.** What are the worst parts about living in a divorced family? Certainly one of the worst feelings is in the beginning, when your dad (or mom) first moves out, or you and your mom (or dad) move out. When that happened, didn't you feel totally awful? And didn't you feel like nobody in the whole world ever felt this awful before? (You may still feel that way now, or your parents may have separated several months ago.)

Wouldn't it have helped — just a tiny little bit — if you had known about other kids who've gone through their parents' divorces? Wouldn't it have helped if you knew how they felt?

Why not write a play about it? Then you and your friends can put on the play in your living room or backyard. Your audience can be some other kid who is just now going through the early stages of his parents' divorce.

When he sees the play, he'll understand better that every kid whose parents get divorced feels the same feelings. And by helping him, you'll feel better too. (Got stage fright? You don't have to have an audience at all. Just writing or acting out the play can help you feel better, too.)

Talk to Someone Who Can Help

Still confused about all of this? Who should you talk to? Who can help you? And how?

There are many people who can help. They can help in different ways. Some can help just by listening. As you pour your feelings out, you'll feel better. Others can help by offering either advice based on common sense, or advice based on their own experience. And some people are experts whose job it is to help people feel better. Here are some people you can think about talking to:

• **Understanding older relatives** — aunts, uncles, grandparents, or others.

- **Your favorite teacher.** This could be your teacher now, a teacher you had in the past, a music teacher, a Sunday School teacher, even a gymnastics teacher you feel comfortable talking to.

- **Your Scoutmaster or Scout troop leader.**

- **Your clergyperson** — priest, rabbi, cantor, minister, pastor, or other.

- **A neighbor** you feel close to and comfortable talking with.

- **A friend of your parents** whom you feel close to and comfortable with.

- **A parent of one of your friends** — someone who makes you feel good inside.

- **Another kid who's been through divorce** with his or her parents. This may be a friend, but it doesn't have to be. A neighbor, classmate, or someone else, even if you don't know him or her very well, can still be very helpful.

If he's been through this himself, he knows what you're going through. He'll probably feel proud to be able to help you. He'll probably also feel bad for you. He's been through what you're going through. He knows how you feel right now. When he says, "I know how awful you feel," he really means it.

He probably also has some more ideas for ways you can help yourself feel better. After all, he knows what worked for him.

• **A parent (besides yours) who has been divorced.** He or she might remember what helped his or her kid. (Maybe he or she can even explain a parent's point of view to you in a way that will help you feel less angry at your own parents.)

• **A psychologist or counselor.** This could be the school psychologist or counselor, or an outside psychologist. Psychologists are trained to help people with their emotional problems. Dealing with your parents' divorce is a very difficult problem to handle. And there is no reason to feel bad about needing a little extra help to handle your emotions, if they're out of control at this time.

5

A Lot of Questions about Divorce . . . with Answers

Mom and Dad didn't say they were getting divorced. They said they were getting separated. But then Dad moved out anyhow. What is "separated," and how is it different from divorce? If they get separated, they can get back together, right?

A separation can mean a couple of different things. Let's talk about what usually happens first.

Once a couple decides that they're better off not being married anymore, one of them usually moves out of the house. At this point, they're not divorced yet — they haven't been to court to see the judge. But they are no longer living together. They are separated.

People often get separated before they get divorced. But that doesn't mean that a couple who gets separated has to get divorced. A couple who no longer wants to be married can't just pop into the court, find a judge, and say, "We've decided to get divorced. Un-marry us." It isn't that easy or that quick.

Sometimes, and in some places, a couple can get a quick divorce. But usually — and especially when kids are involved — it takes a long time. The man and woman will usually each talk to a lawyer . . . a different lawyer for each of them. The two lawyers, or the man and the woman, or all of them together, have a lot of things to decide. I'll tell you what some of them are in a minute.

The final decisions are up to the judge, but the lawyers, and the man and woman, will try to come to an agreement first. If they can't agree on what is known as the "terms of the divorce," they will have to leave it up to the judge. If they can agree on things first it's much easier for everybody. But there are a lot of hard choices to make.

➤ *What kind of choices?*
Here are some of the things they have to decide:

• If the couple owns a house, who is going to keep it after the divorce?

• Who is going to keep each piece of furniture?

• Who is going to keep all the other things that the man and woman own together (such as cars, dishes, TV's, or pictures)?

• Will the man pay the woman some money to help support her? (This money is called alimony. Sometimes when the woman earns more money than the man, she will pay him alimony, but that doesn't happen as often.)

• Will the kids live mostly with their dad or their mom?

• When will the other parent get to see the kids? (What days? For how long?)

• Who gets the kids over vacations and holidays? Will they take turns with each parent?

• How much child support is the father going to pay to the mother? (Child support is money that helps pay for food, clothes, and the other things that kids need.) Or, if the kids are living with the father, the mother might pay child support to him.

• Anything else the couple has to decide in order to end the marriage and be clear on who gets what and who does what.

It takes a while for the couple and their lawyers to try to decide about these choices for how things will be after the divorce. And it usually takes a while before a judge will have time to hear their case and make the final decisions. Also, some states make a couple live apart for a time before they can get a divorce.

When the judge does make the final decisions about the divorce, he or she writes them down on some pages of paper that, all together, are called a "divorce decree." The "divorce decree" tells how the divorce is supposed to work.

➢ *What if the man and woman can't decide about who pays money and how much, and who gets to keep the house, and who the kids will live with, then what?*

Then the judge will decide, and will write it all down in the divorce decree.

Even if the couple has agreed on terms, the judge may decide to do things differently.

• The judge may not agree with the amount of child support or alimony that the couple both agreed to. He or she may think it's not fair to one or the other of them.

• The judge may think the kids should visit with their father or mother more days each month than the couple agreed to.

• The judge may ask the kids which parent they want to live with . . . though that doesn't mean they'll automatically get their wishes. It just means the judge will think about what they say.

After the judge gives the couple their divorce decree, they are legally divorced. But from the time one of them moves out until they get their divorce decree, they are said to be "separated."

➢ *What's the other kind of separation?*

The second kind of separation is called a "trial separation." When a couple gets a trial separation, they know they're not happy living together, but they aren't sure they want to get divorced, either.

This isn't the same kind of "trial" that goes on in a courtroom when someone is accused of a crime. This word "trial" comes from the word "try" and means the couple is going to try living apart from each other. They know they're not happy living together, but they don't know whether they want to get divorced or not. So they try living separately — a trial separation — to see if they like that better than being married to each other.

If they decide they are better off apart than together, then they'll get a divorce. If not, they'll get back together and hope the marriage is happier this time.

But most separations aren't trial separations. Most separations are the first step on the way to a divorce.

➢ *Two of the kids in my class come from divorced families. But one gets to see her dad three nights a week and the other only gets to see his dad once a week. Why is that?*

There could be many different reasons for that. One child's father probably works longer hours than the other, so he doesn't have as much time to see his child. Or maybe he works evenings, and the only time he can see his child is on weekends. Or maybe he and his ex-wife don't live near each other. One of them could have moved to another town after their divorce; not a far-away city, but someplace that's too far to drive on a weekday. Maybe he lives too far from his son to see him more than once a week.

➤ *What if my mom and I move to another city far away?*

Everything I said before would still be true, only in this case, it's you, and not your dad, who moves. You'd still get to go visit him. You'll spend more time with him over vacations instead. Probably you'll get to spend winter or spring break — very possibly both — with him, as well as a good part of your summer vacation.

➤ *My friend's parents are divorced. After the divorce, his mom changed her last name. Is my mom going to change her name?*

Some women change their last names when they get divorced. Usually, they take back their maiden names. (A woman's "maiden name" is the last name she was born with. Her "married name" is the last name of her husband. Most, but not all, women change their last names to their husbands' last names when they get married. And some women take back their maiden names when they get divorced.) A very few women change their last names to something else altogether when they get divorced.

If you have strong feelings about your mom changing her last name, talk to her. She may not be planning to do that at all. And if she is planning to do it, and you don't want her to, she might listen to you. It's worth talking it over. Start by asking if she even plans to do it.

➢ *If she does change her name, her last name won't be the same as mine. Does that mean we're not a family anymore?*

Being a family has to do with love, not with last names. Your mom still loves you, whether or not she has the same last name as you. Your dad still loves you, too. Even if you and he had different last names, he would still love you just as much.

➢ *Does that mean that if my mom changes her last name, I can change mine too?*

That's up to your mom, your dad, the lawyers, and the judge. (Another judge, or the same one who handles the divorce.) Whenever a person changes his or her last name, it has to be approved by a judge. The judge who is in charge of the divorce hearing can take care of changing your last name, too . . . if your parents and their lawyers approve of it.

➤ *Why wouldn't the lawyers approve?*

Your dad and his lawyer might want you to keep your dad's last name. They might make it one of the things the divorce decree says. The judge might write down that your mom can't change your last name.

➤ *What about when I grow up? Can I change it then?*

Certainly, when you're grown up — if you still want to — you can change your last name.

➤ *Mom and Dad used to say that they wouldn't ever get divorced. Why did they say that if it wasn't true?*

They may not have been trying to keep things from you, but didn't even know themselves that things were going to turn out this way. Sometimes it's hard for people to say (even to family), "I just don't know what's going to happen." So, they pretend that everything is OK. Or, maybe they thought things were going to get better. It might not seem fair now, but they probably just didn't want you to worry.

➤ *Why do my parents have to get divorced right now? Everything seems scarier than usual lately. Couldn't they wait a while? I'm having enough trouble already without them getting divorced!*

It's probably because of the divorce that things seem scarier than usual. Think back. When did things start scaring you worse? Was it around the time they told you they were getting a divorce? Or maybe it was when you started hearing them arguing more than they used to? Or when you noticed that things felt more tense around the house?

Lots of times, kids feel that something is wrong without even realizing they know it. Mom and Dad argue more. Or Dad is cold to Mom and gives her one-word answers. Or Mom is barely polite to Dad. The kids might not think about it on the surface, but deep down underneath they can feel that things aren't quite right.

➤ *But I never heard them fight at all!*

Even if Mom and Dad don't fight in front of the kids, the kids hear the strain in their parents' voices. The kids *don't* hear the love in their parents' voices that they used to hear before. Mom and Dad talk to each other much less than they used to. And when they do talk, they don't sound friendly. Even if the kids don't think about it, they somehow realize something is wrong.

Divorce usually has an effect on kids. But even the tensions in the house before the divorce can have an effect. And one thing that kids often notice is that they get scared more easily.

➤ *I don't feel scared during the day, but at night I've been having a lot of bad dreams. Is that because of the divorce?*

Bad dreams are just another way of being scared. Some kids feel scared when they're awake. In other kids, the fear comes out when they're sleeping, as bad dreams, or even nightmares. In a few months you'll probably start feeling less scared. That will mean fewer bad dreams, or none at all. Sometimes it helps to talk about your feelings with someone you trust like your mom or dad (or maybe a grandparent or other relative, if you have a hard time talking to your parents about it right now).

In some kids, fear can show itself in other ways. For instance, some kids who haven't wet their beds since they were two or three years old will suddenly start bedwetting again, even at age nine or ten. It's nothing to be ashamed of. It's just another way of the fear coming out.

Divorce is a very upsetting thing . . . but you *will* get through it.

6

Visiting Your Dad or Mom

It's going to seem strange, the first time you go to visit your dad. (Of course, if you're living with your dad, you'll be visiting your mom. But let's say, for the moment, that you're living with your mom. That's more common.)

Why is it going to seem strange? There are several reasons:

• **The very idea of "visiting Dad" will feel weird.** Dad isn't someone you go to visit! Home is where Dad is, and where Dad belongs. Or at least, that's the way it always was until recently.

• **You may be worried about leaving your mom alone.** If you're ever afraid that your mom or dad will be lonely or sad while you're gone, you can plan to call him or her a time or two while you're away. You probably will miss each other, that's normal. But remember that your parents are adults and you may *care about them*, but it's not your job to *take care of them*. (Plus, your mom or dad may actually enjoy some time alone or with friends!)

• **Your dad will be living in a new place.** This might be a new house or apartment that he's living in by himself, or he might be living with a roommate. He could even have moved back in with his own parents, a brother, or some other relative. But it will probably be some new place that you have never been to before.

• **Chances are, Dad will have gotten some new furniture.** You'll look at it and say, "*That's* not Dad's dresser. That's not Dad's table."

• **On the other hand, some familiar furniture from your home may have gone with Dad to his new home.** You'll look at it and feel funny inside, seeing Dad's familiar workbench in this strange house, or Dad's familiar chair in this new apartment.

• **You and your dad may not know what to say to each other at first.** Because it feels funny to be visiting him, and because the only thing on your mind right now may be, "Why did you and Mom have to get divorced?" you may not think of anything to say when he asks you, "What's new in your life since the last time I saw you?"

◆ ◆ ◆

Jennifer's dad and mom got divorced, and her dad moved to an apartment across town. For two weeks they didn't see each other. Then Jennifer's mom told her that her dad would come by that Saturday to take her to his new place for the weekend.

Jennifer was really excited. So was her dad. They both missed each other and wanted to see each other. For two weeks, they had only talked on the phone. And they hadn't even done that every day.

The day got off to a bad start. To begin with, Jennifer had a daydream, a fantasy that she had replayed over and over in her head for a week. In her fantasy, her dad would walk in the door, take a look at her mom, and kiss her just like always. They would start talking, and before they knew it, they would realize this divorce thing had been a big mistake. Then Jennifer's dad would move back in, and things would be like they had been before.

But it didn't happen like that. When Jennifer's dad got to her house, he was polite to her mom, but he acted like he wasn't happy to be there. He didn't act mean to Jennifer's mom, but he wasn't nice and friendly and loving, either.

Her mom didn't act nice and friendly, either. She was polite, but that was all. She didn't offer him a glass of soda or a cup of coffee. She didn't ask him to come in and sit down. She didn't kiss him hello. The way she asked Jennifer if her bag was all packed, and if she was all ready, it seemed like Jennifer's mom was in a hurry to get Jennifer and her dad out the door quickly.

Jennifer didn't know which of her parents she was more unhappy with. If they didn't start acting nicer to each other, things weren't going to happen the way Jennifer had imagined them.

Jennifer's dad seemed just as glad to rush out of the house as her mom was to get him out of there. Jennifer's parents didn't say much to each other at all. What was wrong with them? Why didn't they talk?!

When they left the house, Jennifer was feeling very inside-out. Nothing was right in the world anymore. On the way to her dad's house, he and Jennifer didn't say much to each other.

When they got to Jennifer's dad's house, he asked her, "Do you want some lunch?" But he didn't have peanut butter and jelly, or American cheese or frozen pizza, or hot dogs.

He offered Jennifer some strange-looking cheese, but it smelled funny, and she made a face. He found some smoked turkey in the fridge, but

Jennifer didn't want that either. Just the name grossed her out.

Finally he found a can of tomato soup. Jennifer didn't hate tomato soup, but she didn't love it, either. She agreed to have it for lunch, but this day seemed to be getting worse by the minute.

Jennifer looked around the new apartment. She saw the painted clay bowl that she had made in kindergarten. Her dad used it to hold paper clips. It was sitting on his new dresser, but it looked so wrong there! It looked so out of place! It belonged on his dresser in her house!

When she went back into the living room, her dad was sitting in his chair. Only, it wasn't the chair he had always sat in at her house. That chair was still there, and it looked so empty without Dad in it. Dad was sitting in this new chair, and that didn't look right either. Jennifer felt more mixed-up inside than ever.

"You may eat at that card table," Jennifer's dad said. She saw that he had set a bowl of soup down on the table in the corner of the living room. At home, she was normally only allowed to eat in the kitchen or the dining room. She thought it was a treat when sometimes her mom let her eat in the living room. But now it just made her feel more turned around.

When she was through eating, her dad said, "Let's talk. Tell me what's new since I saw you last."

For some reason, Jennifer couldn't think of anything. "Nothing," she said, kicking the table a little.

"Something must have happened in the two weeks since I've seen you," her dad said.

The biggest thing to happen in Jennifer's life in the last two weeks was that her dad had moved out of the house. But she didn't think she needed to tell him that! He already knew he and her mom were getting a divorce.

"Come on. Share some news with me," her dad said. But Jennifer couldn't think of anything else.

"What's going on in school?" her dad asked. Jennifer usually liked to talk about school. When her dad had lived with her, she used to think of a lot of news from school that she wanted to share with him. But now he was asking her to sit there and talk even though there was nothing she particularly wanted to talk about.

"I can't think of anything," she said. He looked at her. She looked at him. But her mind was blank. She couldn't think of any news. And the more they just looked at each other, the stranger she felt.

Finally, her dad started asking her specific questions, such as, "What did you study in Science this week?" and "Did you get any interesting new music to learn in the school band?" and, "Can you do the new beam dismount that you were working on in gymnastics?"

Jennifer felt she was being drilled with questions. Why was he interrogating her? "Cut it out!" she snapped. Immediately she felt guilty for yelling at her dad, but she didn't apologize. She felt like he deserved to have her be mean to him. It was his fault for asking so many questions.

The whole thing was his fault anyhow; if he hadn't moved out, she wouldn't be sitting in this strange place, trying to think of something to say, and feeling uncomfortable with her own father.

"What are we going to do this afternoon?" Jennifer finally asked.

"I thought we'd just spend the afternoon together," her dad said.

"But what are we going to do?" Jennifer repeated.

"I — I had thought we'd just talk, catch up on what's been happening the last couple of weeks," her dad said.

Jennifer wanted to roll her eyes, but she knew that would get her in trouble; it was already obvious that her dad's plan wasn't going to work.

Jennifer's mom had suggested she bring her Parcheesi™ game and a book with her. Jennifer *and her dad played two games of Parcheesi™, but then they both were bored with it. Jennifer didn't feel like reading, so she turned on the TV.*

"I thought we were going to visit together," her dad said. "I haven't seen you in two weeks!"

"Well, what do you want to do?" Jennifer asked. But her dad didn't have any specific ideas. When he'd lived with her and her mother, they could have gone out and worked in the garden together. But there was no garden here. They could have gone next door and visited Mr. Crawford and his dog. But Jennifer's dad didn't know any of his new neighbors yet. They could have climbed up in the tree house together. But there was no tree house here. They could have gone into Jennifer's room and made collages together. But Jennifer didn't have a room here, and there were no good magazines to cut up for collages.

Jennifer stayed over at her dad's house that night. He showed her that the new sofa he had bought could turn into a bed. He said it was a bed just for her. But she didn't feel very comfortable in it. She kept wishing she were home, where things felt more normal. It took her a long time to fall asleep.

Sunday morning, Jennifer's dad made a big pancake breakfast. Jennifer enjoyed the pancakes and bacon, and her dad watched cartoons on TV with her. Then they went to the zoo. She enjoyed that too. She finally started to relax.

While they were at the zoo, things seemed more normal. They had been to the zoo plenty of times before. Sometimes they went with her mom and sometimes just the two of them. So being at the zoo with her dad felt good. It was a familiar thing to do. It didn't feel new or strange.

But then it started to rain. "We'd better go home," Jennifer's dad said. At the word "home," Jennifer felt good at first, but then she realized that when he said "home," he meant his new apartment. Jennifer felt tricked. That wasn't home! It wasn't her home, and she didn't want it to be his home either!

But they popped popcorn and played a game of Monopoly™. Jennifer won the game, and that made her feel happy. The popcorn tasted good. Suddenly it was 5:30.

"I'd better get you home," Jennifer's dad said. Just when she was starting to feel a little bit comfortable in the new apartment, he was sending her back home! Jennifer felt cheated all over again.

When she got back home, she was surprised to find that she even felt out of place there. Her mother asked her how she'd enjoyed the weekend, but Jennifer just wanted to go to her

*room and listen to music and play with her toys.
She didn't want to answer any questions. Coming
home felt just as weird as going to Daddy's place
had felt, and Jennifer didn't like that.*

*After an hour in her room, Jennifer felt normal
again. And two weeks later, when she went back
to her dad's, she didn't feel as strange in his
apartment. It still didn't feel like anyplace she
could call "home," but she didn't feel as weird
and out of place there.*

*And, when her dad asked her what was new,
she actually thought of some things to tell him.*

Sometimes parents are so wrapped up in their own
problems of going through a divorce that they forget it
isn't easy on the kids either. On the other hand, the
same thing is true for kids. Sometimes kids are so
involved in how bad they feel over the divorce that
they forget it isn't easy on their parents, either.

➤ *But Mom and Dad were the ones who wanted the
divorce. I didn't ask for this. So they must be happy with
it. But I'm not.*

Sometimes you know what the best thing is to do,
but you're still not happy about the decision. Your
mom and dad may have decided it was best to get a
divorce, but that doesn't necessarily mean they're
totally happy about it. If they were fighting, or just not
getting along, things may be more peaceful now, or
easier, but they still could be lonely.

Money may be a bigger problem now than before, and your parents could be worried about that. Raising a child by yourself isn't as easy without another parent there to help you. And being a "visiting" parent isn't as enjoyable as living with your child.

Many things are different now from how they were before. Isn't it a little hard for you to get used to all these changes? Well, it's hard for them, too. So try to be easy on your parents. This is a difficult time for all of you. That doesn't mean that you should hide your feelings, or act like someone you're not. It just means that it's good to try to understand how the people you care about feel, and not to be too hard on them.

And when you go to visit your dad (or your mom, if you're living with your dad now), remember that he (or she) feels as awkward as you do.

Things your dad (or mom) is probably concerned about:

• "Will you be comfortable when you come to my new place?"

• "How can I help you feel at home here?"

• "How are we going to spend a whole weekend without you getting bored?"

• "Can I cook the foods you like?"

• "Are you still angry at me about the divorce?"

Things you can do to make visiting weekends easier:

- **Bring toys, games, and books from home.** Bring both things you can do by yourself that you enjoy, and things you can do with the parent you're visiting.

- **Bring a few familiar things that will make you feel more comfortable,** like your pillow, or a favorite stuffed animal, cassette tape or CD. Most of the things that you'll bring you'll take back with you when you return home, but also bring a few things you can leave behind at your dad's (or mom's) new house. The things you leave there will make the new house seem more familiar when you visit it, as well as giving you more things to do while you're there.

- **Make a list of exciting, interesting, or other important things that happen to you between visits.** Your list can be simple:

    Got in fight with Lee.

    Got "A" on spelling test.

    Joined school chorus.

    New kid in our class.

    Helped mom bake pie.

    Got badge in Scouts.

You don't have to write down details. You'll remember most of them. But when your dad asks, "What's happened since I saw you last?" you'll have a list to remind you of things you can tell him. Instead of saying, "Nothing," you'll have answers.

It isn't always easy to fill your dad in on what's happened to you when you might not feel like talking right then, but the list will help.

• **Try keeping a journal or diary.** Not only is it a good way to let your feelings out, it's also a record of what's going on in your life. You can always look back over it to remind yourself of things you might want to talk about with your dad or mom. Remember that it's just for you.

• **Ask your dad if you may invite one of your friends over to visit you at his house.** Sometimes having a friend over makes things feel more normal. But remember, your dad hasn't seen you since your last visit, and he wants to spend time with you. If you do have a friend over to visit, don't leave your dad out. Don't spend the whole weekend ignoring your dad. You can do things all together.

• **On the other hand, you and your dad don't have to spend every single minute together,** whether you've got a friend over or not. You each need some time to yourselves.

➤ *Why are the rules always changing?*

Here's another thing you need to know: The rules may be different in your two parents' houses. It will take some getting used to. And sometimes you'll make a mistake. (So will your parents.) But don't expect one parent to go along with the other parent's rules. You can ask to have the same privileges at each parent's house, but complaining about the rules is probably not going to convince your parents to change them.

◆ ◆ ◆

Jason lives with his dad but visits his mom every Saturday. The first time he slept at his mom's house, his mom made him go to bed at 9:00, the same as at his dad's house. But after a few months, his mom decided he was old enough to stay up till 9:30.

When Jason went home to his dad's house, he said, "Mom lets me stay up till 9:30. I want to stay up till 9:30 here too, OK?"

"No, that's not OK," his dad said. "I think 9:30 is too late for you to go to bed. If your mom wants to let you stay up late, that's her business, but in my house you'll continue to go to bed at 9:00 until you're older."

"You're mean!" Jason said angrily. "That's not fair! I should get to stay up till 9:30 like at Mom's house!"

"Watch your tone of voice, or you're going to

be sent to your room," Jason's dad said.

"You don't love me as much as Mom does,"
Jason answered. "And I love Mom better than I
love you."

We can understand why Jason felt upset and angry, but the words he said were really hurtful to his dad. He really knew, deep inside him, that having more privileges at his mom's house didn't mean she loved him better than his dad did. And he didn't really love his mom better than he loved his dad. He just was angry at his dad at that moment.

What could Jason have done, instead of lashing out at his dad? How about if he tried to look at the extra privileges at his mom's house as a treat: "Oh wow — at Mom's house I get to stay up late!" That's looking at the positive side of things, and it would leave Jason feeling much better inside. And he could have told his dad — without yelling — that he was disappointed about the 9:00 bedtime. He might also have asked his dad, "How much older?" so he had something to look forward to in the future. Trying to work with his dad, instead of fighting with him, will help both of them to feel better. Don't you think Jason will feel much happier that way than if he thinks, "Why isn't Dad as nice to me as Mom is?"

◆ ◆ ◆

Caitlin has to take out the garbage after dinner whenever she visits her dad. It's the only chore her dad expects of her, but since she's only at her dad's house twice a week, she often forgets. At home, at her mom's house, she has other chores to do. But since Caitlin's mom doesn't expect her to take out the garbage, Caitlin doesn't always remember when she's at her dad's.

One Wednesday night, when Caitlin was at her father's house, she forgot the garbage again. She had forgotten it on Saturday night, too. Caitlin's dad got angry at her. "Why can't you ever take out the garbage?" he demanded. "It's not like I ask you to do that much. One simple thing! But you keep ignoring it. I shouldn't have to ask you every time."

Caitlin started to sniffle. "Why won't you let me do the dishes instead, like I do at home?" she asked. "Or I could help with your laundry. I help Mom with her laundry."

"Why is it such a problem to take out the garbage?" Caitlin's dad answered. "One little chore. Just one." Then he walked out of the room before she could answer. She was left feeling hurt and angry, and her little sniffles became big tears.

Caitlin and her dad were both a little bit wrong and a lot right. Caitlin's dad uses paper plates a lot. He also has a dishwasher and uses it. So, he really doesn't need her to help him with the dishes. He has a cleaning service come in once a week to clean his house, and they do the laundry, too. So he doesn't need Caitlin's help with the laundry either. But the garbage does need to be taken out to the trash can every night after dinner. Besides, a very important part of helping out is to help where you are really needed, not just when it's convenient, or easy.

It's fair for Caitlin's dad to ask her to take out the garbage. But it's understandable that she would forget it.

Caitlin doesn't object to taking out the garbage. She just needs to be reminded. After three months of having her dad and mom living apart, Caitlin really should remember the garbage without a reminder. But, on the other hand, it's not so awful for her dad to have to remind her, either.

What could Caitlin have done differently?

We can understand why she started crying. She felt her father was being unfair to her. She hadn't refused to take out the garbage. She just didn't remember.

What if she had said, "Dad, I don't mind taking out the garbage, but I need some help in remembering." Then, Caitlin's dad would have better understood that Caitlin was willing to help, just forgetful.

What could Caitlin's dad do to help her remember?

• He could remind her every night that she's at his house for a month or so, till she's used to doing it. Then he could ask her if she's ready to try remembering the garbage without help.

• He could leave a note or other reminder for her somewhere. If she always has a glass of milk after dinner, he could leave a note taped to the fridge. If she usually watches TV after dinner, he could leave a note on the TV.

• He could make a game of taking out the garbage, leaving notes in unusual places, or putting a quarter under the trash bag, or leaving her a message on the answering machine, or putting the trash bag on her bed, or making up a song about the trash. She'd probably remember that.

If Caitlin's dad doesn't think of helpful reminders for her, Caitlin could suggest one of these ideas to him, or ask if they could have a "brainstorming session" to come up with good suggestions together. (Brainstorming is where people get together and think of lots and lots of ideas — they can be stupid, or silly, or good, it really doesn't matter — and usually at least a few of the ideas can really work. It can be fun and a good way to come up with answers that everyone can be happy with.)

The rules are often different between one house and the other when your parents don't live together. One parent allows you to do something the other one doesn't. One parent asks you to do a chore that the other one doesn't. That doesn't make one parent "right" and the other one "wrong."

Occasionally, a parent might really ask you to do something that you think is too hard at your age. If this happens, you can sit down and try to talk out the problem. Explain that you think you're not old enough, or tall enough, or strong enough . . . whatever is the case.

But most of the time, there is nothing wrong with them expecting different things of you. It's just a question of two different parents having two different rules. (Just as you might have to learn new rules when you're visiting at a friend's house.) One parent will allow a privilege that the other doesn't. And one will give you a responsibility that the other doesn't. Nobody is right or wrong. They are just different.

Don't play one parent against the other. Don't say, "But Dad lets me . . ." or, "But Mom doesn't make me . . ." That might only irritate them, and certainly won't help you get what you want. Look at extra privileges in one house as treats. If you really have trouble remembering the differences in rules from one house to the other, ask for help. And if you think either parent is being unfair, talk it out calmly with that parent.

There are always going to be things you like better about one house than the other . . . Maybe:

• When Dad cooks chicken, it comes out dry and tasteless. Mom's roast chicken is one of your favorite foods. But Dad cooks homemade pizza that's better than the take-out pizza Mom gets . . . and he lets you help him make it.

• Dad lets you sleep out on his balcony in warm weather. Mom doesn't let you camp out in the backyard. But Mom will take you to the ice rink and go skating with you, and Dad never takes you there.

• Dad will take you out for doughnuts in the morning. Mom says they're not good for you and won't buy them. But Mom lets you have a big after-school snack, while Dad says you can't because it will spoil your dinner.

• Dad insists you do all your homework before dinner when you go to his house on a school night. Mom lets you play outside for half an hour first. But Mom gives you one major chore every week that takes about an hour. Dad has no such rule.

It's not that either parent is nicer. It's certainly not that either parent loves you more. It's just that they're different people and have different rules. Don't fight it.

➢ *But why can't they just treat me the same?*

◆ ◆ ◆

Melissa's dad and mom got divorced, and her dad rented a house not far from Melissa and her mom's house. Every Thursday and Saturday, Melissa goes to her dad's house.

Melissa's dad won't let Melissa watch one of her favorite TV programs. He thinks it's not a good show for a child to watch. He also asks her to put away the dinner dishes after he washes them.

Melissa minds missing her favorite show. But she knows that saying, "Mommy always let me," won't earn her father's permission to watch it. She tried begging and pleading, but that didn't work. She tried talking about it calmly, but her father held firm. He believes that the show is not a good one for Melissa.

Melissa finally dropped the subject. She wasn't happy, but she knew she wasn't going to win this one. In another six months, she'll tell her dad, "I'm six months older, now. Will you think about letting me watch that show?"

Maybe he will, and maybe he won't. It's worth trying. And if he still says, "No," she knows she can ask him again in another six months. As long as she doesn't make an unpleasant scene out of asking, her dad won't mind if she brings the subject up again in six months.

As for the dishes, that's another story. Melissa had a good reason for not wanting to put the dishes away. At her house, the cabinets are a little lower. At her dad's house, she has trouble reaching the shelf where the glasses go.

"Dad, I can barely stretch that far," she explained to him. "And besides, I'm afraid I'm going to drop a glass, the way I have to reach to put them away." Melissa asked if she could trade chores. Would her father give her a different chore to do instead? One that she was better able to do?

Instead, her father bought a step-stool. Melissa can carefully climb on it to put the glasses away. She isn't uncomfortable. She isn't afraid of dropping a glass.

Melissa didn't say, "Mom doesn't make me put the dishes away." She had a good reason for not wanting to do this particular chore. When she explained the reason to her dad, he found a way to overcome the problem.

The rules are going to be different from house to house. "Mom doesn't make me," or "Dad lets me" aren't good reasons for asking to change the rules. But if you have a real reason to question one of the rules, tell your parent that reason calmly and honestly — without whining or yelling. And if you don't have a good reason, get used to the fact that the rules are going to change from one house to the other.

7

Staying "Close" to Far-away Parents

Sometimes, after a divorce, one parent or the other moves to someplace far away. This may be because he or she got a good job, but it's in another town. Sometimes, too, a person who's getting divorced decides to move back to his or her home town (where he or she grew up), or to a place where there are a lot of friends or family.

If a man or woman now has kids to raise without the help of a spouse, moving near family can help. Moving back near his or her own mom or dad means that Grandma or Grandpa can help watch the kids while Mom or Dad works. Or Grandma and Grandpa can help in other ways, such as carpooling, shopping, or with homework. Sometimes all that's needed is for them to be around to offer advice and companionship to Mom or Dad, and grandmotherly (or grandfatherly) love to the kids.

When the dad gets custody, raising the kids near Grandma gives them a motherly figure to turn to when they want one. And when the mom has custody, it's nice to have Grandpa to turn to when Dad's not around.

Sometimes, of course, it's the non-custodial parent (the parent who does not have custody) who moves. The move may be because of a job change. It could be for other reasons, too. A divorced person might choose to go to college, for example, in order to get a better job or a new career after graduating.

Now think about this: Mr. And Mrs. Zyxx have gotten divorced. They had a group of friends they used to spend time with. Since the divorce, the friends might be taking sides. They might feel Mrs. Zyxx was right to divorce Mr. Zyxx (or the other way around). If they take her side, he isn't going to feel comfortable spending time with those friends, and vice versa.

Even if they don't take sides, Mr. Zyxx might not feel comfortable with those friends anymore. He is no longer married, no longer comfortable with his old friends, and really wants to just start all over somewhere else. He might very well move to another city at that point. Of course, the same could happen to Mrs. Zyxx.

There are lots of reasons why divorced people sometimes move. We won't list every one of them here, because *why* people move isn't that important to you. What's important is that *most divorced parents stay in the same town as before, but a number of them do move somewhere else.*

So supposing one of your parents moves? For what we're going to talk about, it doesn't matter whether it's the custodial parent (the one you're living with) who moves, or your other parent. It doesn't matter whether it's your mom or your dad who moves. But you find yourself living in one town while one of your parents is living in another town.

Again, I want to say that *it is not terribly likely that this will happen. In most cases it doesn't.* But if it does happen to you, what will you do?

Most important, you *will* get to see your other parent. It probably won't be every weekend, or even every other weekend. But maybe you'll spend more time with him (or her) over holidays, instead.

What about all the time between visits, though?

Some Ways to Keep in Touch

You don't have to be out of touch with your out-of-town parent. (Let's say it's your dad, for the moment.) You might be sad because you won't get to feel his arms around you, won't be able to kiss his cheek, won't be able to play Monopoly™ with him. But there are lots of ways the two of you can stay in touch. What are some of them?

• **One of the oldest ways to keep in touch is writing letters.** You can write to your dad every night, or once a week, or just as often as you feel like it. Tell him everything exciting or interesting that happened that day.

Did you get an "A" on a test (or a dreaded "F")? Did you get in an argument with another kid, make a new friend, have a substitute teacher in your class, finish a book report on Eskimos, find an unusually shaped rock, or see something especially funny on TV? Put it in the letter.

Going on a class field trip? If there's a gift shop where you're going, buy a postcard. (They usually don't cost much money.) The picture on the card will help you describe your trip, and your dad will be glad that you thought of him.

Even if your letter or note is just a couple of sentences long, your dad will be thrilled to get it. (He'll miss you at least as much as you'll miss him.) And if he writes you a letter back for every letter you send him, think of all the mail you'll be getting — from Dad!

• **Send e-mail.** If you and your dad both have computers, do you each have an on-line service? (If not, suggest to your parents that it might be worth getting on-line service for both computers.) You can send each other e-mail, letters that will be delivered almost the minute they are sent. And at least one service (America Online) lets you "talk" (type) back and forth to each other while you're both on-line. (It's called "instant messaging.") You can read your dad's words as soon as he types them, and you can answer him right away. (Plus, the cost of the online service is often cheaper than making lots of long-distance telephone calls.)

• **Keep a journal.** Instead of writing a letter every night (or many nights), you can write your reports of each day's happenings in a small blank book or on loose-leaf pages. (This is not the same book as your private diary — that one is only for yourself.) Once a week, send the book or pages to your dad.

Of course, the more details you give him, the more he'll enjoy it. But if you aren't much of a writer, you may not feel like thinking up long sentences describing the day's events. Fine. You can at least jot short notes mentioning the things that happened each day: "Played softball after school. Rode my bike to Lincoln Park. Found a robin's nest in the oak tree. Baked oatmeal raisin cookies with Mom. No homework today! And school's out for vacation in just three more weeks. Hooray!"

• **Long-distance calls.** You and your dad certainly want to hear each other's voice. Long-distance calls cost money, but if you keep them short, you can afford to call more often. On the other hand, you could call only once a week and talk for much longer. You might want to write down a few things you'd like to mention to your dad beforehand, so that you don't forget them when you're on the phone together.

• **Your dad can get an 800 number.** Long-distance phone companies now offer 800 numbers to individuals, not just big businesses. You may already know that when a person dials an 800 number — a number with either "800" or "888" or "877" as the area code — it's a free call. (Of course *somebody* has to pay for the call. The cost is paid by the person who *gets* the call, instead of the person who *dials* the call.)

Maybe your mom has limited the number of times you may call your dad, because she can't afford for you to run up the phone bill. But if your dad can afford to get an 800 number, you can call him as often as he'll let you. It won't cost your mom anything. (It *will* cost your dad every time you call.)

Your dad might not even know about "Personal 800 numbers" yet. But you can suggest to him that he get one.

• **Tape your news.** Maybe you prefer "talking your news" to writing it, but your parents can't afford for you to make long-distance calls often. And maybe your dad doesn't want, or can't afford, an 800 number. In that case, all you need is a tape recorder and a few cassette tapes.

Any kind will do. It can be a little cassette recorder, a boom box, or the tape deck on a big stereo, as long as it has a microphone. This can be a plug-in mike or a built-in mike. Your dad will need to have a cassette tape player too, in order to listen to your tapes. And, in order to send "taped letters" back to you, telling you what's going on with him and how much he misses you, he'll need a cassette recorder with a microphone, too.

Your best bet is probably to tape a few minutes' conversation every night and mail off the tape once a week. Just as with the journal or letters, you can tell your dad a lot or a little about each day's events.

Turn on the tape recorder and say, "Today is Monday" (or whatever day it is). Then start telling your dad all the interesting stuff that happened today.

You'll probably just want to talk into the tape recorder as if you were talking to him. (If that feels funny and you're not comfortable, here's a trick: Close your eyes, try not to think about the tape recorder, imagine your dad's face, and then just talk as if you were talking to him.)

But you don't have to talk as if you were having a conversation with him. You can be funny, if you want, and pretend you're a TV newscaster. If your name, for instance, is Pat, you can start the tape with, "This is radio station W-P-A-T." (If your name is longer than three letters, don't worry. You aren't a real radio station, so you can be W-L-E-S-L-I-E if you want to be. And if you live west of the Mississippi River, use a "K" instead of a "W," as real radio and TV stations do.)

Then you can say something like, "Here are the news headlines for March 28th." Continue giving the news, talking about yourself as if you were someone else: "Leslie Gordon amazed Ms. Fisher's fifth grade today by remembering all the verses to 'America the Beautiful' in assembly. Sports news: Leslie Gordon scored three baskets in gym today. And here is your Centreville weather report: It's been cloudy all day, with temperatures only in the high 50s, but tomorrow is supposed to be sunny and warmer. In other news, Molasses, the Gordon family's pet dog, dug under the fence and escaped. She was found by a woman three blocks away. The woman looked at Molasses's tag, saw who she belonged to, and returned her to her worried family."

It doesn't matter whether you make your tape sound like a radio news broadcast or just talk to your dad the way you would if you were both in the same room. The important thing is to tell him what's going on in your life.

• **"A picture is worth a thousand words."** That's how the old saying goes. The truth is, neither one can replace the other. Pictures alone can't replace your words telling Dad all about the things that are going on in your life. But naturally, your dad wants to see what you look like between visits, too.

You're growing. How tall have you gotten to be? Has the length or style of your hair changed? In what other ways do you look different from the last time he saw you? Did you get new clothes? Did your sports team, the school band, your new Scout troop, or some other group you belong to get new uniforms or equipment? Send pictures!

Get your mom, or your friends, or some other relatives to take pictures of you. Then send them to your dad. Let him see pictures of you as you look now. Pictures that show something more than you just standing there are better. The picture might show you swinging a bat, sharing a soda with your new best friend, or sitting at the new desk in your bedroom. Your dad will see that you're playing softball, what your new friend looks like, that you've got a new desk. He'll not only see what you look like these days, he'll learn something more about your life.

- **Pictures that move are even better.** So get your mom, a friend, or another relative to take some pictures of you with a videotape recorder, if possible. These are more expensive, so this isn't an activity for every day, or every week. Maybe not even every month. But from time to time — or on special occasions — record yourself on a videotape and send it to your dad.

• **Computers can send pictures almost instantly.**
The newest computers can connect to cameras that
allow you to send pictures by e-mail. You can sit in
front of the computer and your dad can see you at the
same time, or later in a message you send. If you and
your dad have new computers, check it out!

Along with the suggestions I've just made, you can send
your dad little things that will help him keep feeling
connected to you. Did you recently make a collage in
art class in school? Did your neighbor invite you into his
woodworking shop and help you to make a pair of
bookends? Did you make fudge in the kitchen last
weekend? Send him the collage, the bookends, some
pieces of fudge. Did you buy him a shirt with the name
of his favorite team on it? That's nice . . . now mail it
off to him. It will make him feel good to know you
were thinking about him.

   And you know that, when he gets it, he'll be thinking
about you, too.

8

Parents Are Human, Too

When you were really little, you probably thought your parents were perfect. Your mom never made mistakes; your dad could do no wrong. As you grew older, you learned this wasn't so. You began to realize that, although they might be wonderful parents, "wonderful" is not the same thing as "perfect."

Your parents are human, and they make mistakes like anyone else. They try to do the right thing, and most of the time they succeed, but sometimes they mess up just like anyone else. And when people are under a lot of stress, they're even more likely to make mistakes.

Divorce puts people under a lot of stress. This is a difficult time for both your mom and your dad. (I know . . . it's a difficult time for you, too. And you didn't ask for them to get divorced, which makes it even harder on you. This was their decision, not yours. But believe me, it's not easy for them, either.)

This chapter is going to discuss a few mistakes parents make. I'm talking about mistakes that involve kids. If your parents make one of these mistakes, you can speak up — gently! — and point out that they're being unfair to you.

➤ *What are some of the mistakes that parents make?*

One very common mistake is that **parents sometimes use their kids as spies.** I don't mean that they're going to send you to Russia to see what their army is doing. I mean that your mom and your dad might start asking you a lot of questions about each other. It's very understandable. It's very common. But it's still wrong.

I don't mean questions like, "Did you have a good time at Dad's house?" Or, "How is Mom feeling?" Or, "What did you and Mom do while you were visiting her?" Or, "What did Dad fix for dinner?" Those questions are certainly harmless. They are not "spying" questions.

But suppose your mom and dad are arguing over money. Maybe your dad was late paying the child support or alimony check to your mom. You might or might not know that he was late paying the check. But your mom might now be wondering if he's really short of money, as he says he is.

The next time you go to his house, she might ask you, "Did he spend a lot of money on you this weekend?"

Or, she might ask, "Has Daddy bought a lot of new furniture for his new place?" (Naturally, if you're living with your father, then he is just as likely to ask that kind of question when you come back from visiting your mom. And, of course, the parent you're visiting might ask questions about the parent you live with.)

Divorced parents usually start dating other people sooner or later. (We'll discuss dating in another chapter.) And that's another thing that their ex-husbands and ex-wives get very curious about. Often a mom will ask her kids, "Did Daddy have any women visiting him while you were there?" Or "Did you see any women's clothes hanging in his closet?" Or a more direct question, "Do you know if Daddy has a new girlfriend yet?"

And a dad is just as likely to ask that kind of question when his kids come to visit. "Is your mom seeing any men?" he might ask. Or, if he's trying not to be too obvious about it, he might ask, "Who's been visiting the house lately?"

That doesn't sound like such a bad question, does it? But the dad who asks it might not really be interested in which relatives or old friends have been visiting the house. He is probably more interested in whether any new men have been visiting.

In fact, sometimes it's hard to figure out the difference between an all-right question and a not-so-all-right question. But any time you think your mom or dad is using you to find out what the other parent is doing, speak up. You can politely say something like, "I'd rather you ask Dad [or Mom] that question. I don't like carrying stories from one house to the other." Or, "Please leave me out of the middle. If you want to know something about Dad, please ask him, not me." Or, "I'm not comfortable answering questions about Mom. It makes me feel disloyal. Please ask her if you want to know about her." This is not being impolite, just honest. Remember, you don't need to answer any question that feels like spying.

It's real easy to let yourself be used as a spy. When your dad asks you for information about your mom, and you know the answer, he may thank you or even praise you. Even if he doesn't, we all feel good when we know the answer to a question we're asked. That's normal.

When your mom asks you a question about your dad, and you answer her, you feel you're being helpful, useful. Everyone likes feeling useful. Everyone likes helping his or her mom.

And if your mom or dad thanks you a lot, or praises you for giving information, it's real easy to be caught up in what starts to feel like a game. "Let's see how much I can find out about Dad for Mom." "Let's see how important I can be to Dad by telling him stuff he wants to hear about Mom."

Don't fall into that trap! No matter how helpful or important you feel when you're carrying information, remember, *it's not a good thing to spy on your own parent. Also the parent who is asking you the questions is not being fair to you.* And that's not a good thing for him or her to do.

So don't answer any questions that don't feel right, or that seem to be asking for more information than you think you should be giving.

> *What other mistakes do divorced parents make?*

They use their kids to carry messages. Certain kinds of messages are OK, of course. Suppose your dad always picks you up at your mom's house on Sundays, but not always at the exact same time. When he drops you off this Sunday, he might say, "Tell your mom I'll get you at one o'clock next week." That's usually an OK message.

But suppose your dad wants to change his date to see you. Suppose he always sees you Saturday morning, but next week he wants to pick you up Friday before dinner and have you stay overnight. These changes may not always be OK with your mom. She may have other plans for you that day. It's not OK, then, for your dad to say, "Tell your mom I'll pick you up Friday evening next week." He needs to discuss it with her.

And your mom should not ask you to "Tell your father that the child support check is late, and I need it." It's not your responsibility to carry a message like that; your parents need to work it out between themselves.

You should not have to carry these kinds of messages:

• **Messages that could start fights or cause hurt feelings.** Sometimes it's hard to know if the message could be a problem. If you're not sure about it, it's OK to say, "Maybe you and Mom can talk about that. I wouldn't feel right saying that to her."

• **Messages that require answers, even if they're perfectly nice messages.** Do you know the game "telephone?" One person says something like, "Brian ate scrambled eggs," and it gets whispered around until it changes to something silly like, "Ryan's chair has eighty legs!" It really doesn't do any good to carry this kind of message, because it only goes halfway. In other words, the parent asking the question still won't have an answer until you bring it back, and the message has a good chance of getting mixed up on the way.

• **Messages that criticize the other person.** You can say, "Those are words that should come from you, not me. I couldn't say that to him (her)."

- **Messages about money.** Whether the message is about an alimony or child support check, or bills that need paying, people do often fight about money, so it's better not to get stuck in the middle here. Again, you can say, "I think you and Dad need to talk about that."

- **Messages about schedule changes.** As I mentioned before, scheduling (vacations or visitations) needs to be talked about between parents. It's their responsibility to agree on schedule changes, not yours.

- **Messages about personal habits or relationships.** For example, if your mom asks you to tell your dad that she's been dating someone (or even that she hasn't been dating anyone), that's a message that could cause trouble. You can say that, "If you want Dad to know that, I think you should tell him yourself."

- **Any message you're not comfortable repeating to your other parent.** These could be messages that sound like gossip or rumors, or that you're afraid might hurt or anger your other parent. Be honest: "I'm not comfortable saying that to Mom. Maybe you can tell her that yourself."

If your dad asks you to "Tell your mom that my sister just had another baby," that's an OK message because it's just an interesting fact that you're passing along. But if your dad says, "Tell your mom I don't like her going out so often and leaving you with a sitter so much," that's not an OK message. If he has a problem with something your mom is doing, he needs to discuss it directly with her. It's not your place to carry that kind of message.

➢ *Are there even more mistakes parents make?*

Sometimes they lean on their kids too much. Or they try to turn them into friends. Now, if you see that your mom is feeling sad, it's certainly nice if you cheer her up. But it doesn't help for her to cry and complain to you when your dad does something that upsets her. You can say to her, "Mom, that's between you and Dad. I don't want to hear it. He's still my father."

Not all complaints are about the other parent. Sometimes, because he or she doesn't have a husband or wife to complain to about everyday life, a parent will complain to his or her kids instead. A certain amount of that is OK. There's no reason your mom shouldn't tell you, "I had a rough day at work today." There's no reason your dad can't sometimes say, "Mr. Smith is a difficult boss to work for." But he shouldn't expect you to listen to a whole long story every time he has a bad day.

They shouldn't recite for you a whole list of their current problems. If they do, you can gently say, "It would be better for you to tell that to one of your friends. I'm just a kid." Or you could say, "Why don't you tell one of your friends? They could give you good advice on what to do. I can't. I'm a kid."

➤ *Parents make a lot of mistakes, don't they? Are there any more?*

Punishing you for the other parent's mistake. Sometimes, when a parent is late paying child support, the other parent says, "If you don't pay the support money, you can't see the kids this weekend." It's understandable that the parent who isn't getting what she (or he) deserves would want to take it out on the other parent. But in this case, it isn't fair.

The reason is that you are getting hurt as much as your other (non-paying) parent is.

Assume you live with your mom, and your dad is late with the check. By keeping your dad from seeing you, your mom is also keeping you from seeing your dad. And that's not fair to you.

If your mom asks you to tell your dad he can't see you, that's even worse. Now your mom is, in a way, punishing you because your dad didn't pay on time, and she's asking you to carry a message. If your dad calls on Wednesday to tell you he'll see you on Saturday at 10:00, your mom might say, "Tell him he's not getting you unless I have his check first."

Oops! She's made a mistake. You can tell her, "Please get on the phone and tell him what you want to say. It's not fair for me to carry messages like that. Anyhow, you're really punishing me, too. He's still my father, and I want to see him. It's not right for me to suffer just because he messed up." Of course you don't have to use exactly those words, but that's the general idea you want to get across to your mom.

It might not be easy to say "No" to parents who want you to spy or to carry messages. It's nice to feel your parents can count on you. It's nice to feel helpful. It's nice to feel important. But if your other parent realizes you've been spying, or if your other parent is unhappy with the messages you carry, he or she will not be very happy with you. And you won't feel as good, or as happy, or as important anymore. In fact, you're likely to feel really unhappy.

So, you can avoid the whole problem by not being part of it. Their disagreement doesn't have to become yours. Politely say you don't want to get involved. Remember, your mom and dad don't want to hurt you. But they're human, and human beings make mistakes. Still, you don't have to let their mistakes be your mistakes.

9

A Quick Peek Ahead

No one can say what will happen in the future in your family, but there are some things that are pretty likely. They happen in lots of families!

➤ *My friend's mom is divorced, and she's dating now. Is my mom going to do that too?*

Probably. Once she's divorced from your dad, there's no reason she shouldn't date. Your dad will probably begin dating, too. They may not start dating other people right away. Some people are ready soon after divorce. Others need some time before they're ready. But sooner or later, it's almost certain to happen.

➤ *Does that mean she's going to be leaving me alone all the time?*

If you're not old enough to stay by yourself, she'll certainly get a sitter. Or she might arrange for you to spend the night at a friend's, at your grandma's, or someplace else fun, where you're comfortable.

But I'd guess the main thing bothering you isn't really staying alone. It's the whole idea of your mom dating someone — someone who isn't your dad. You probably feel she's being disloyal. It feels wrong to you. But it's a normal thing that happens after a divorce.

Your mom and dad aren't married anymore. That's a tough thing for you to accept, but you're going to have to get used to it. They're going to begin dating other people. And that's OK.

➤ *Suppose she marries one of them? I don't want some strange man in the house!*

Again, I think what's on your mind is mainly loyalty. Only, this time I think it's your own loyalty you're worried about. I think you're concerned about whether it would be disloyal to your own dad for you to be nice to someone else. Someone who seems to be taking his place.

No one can take your dad's place. He's still your dad. He always will be. But if your mom gets married again, you can still have a good relationship with her new husband. He can be there for you when your own dad's not around. He can do some of the things with you that you liked to do with your dad before he moved out.

Right now, the idea of having another man in the house, trying to be a "second dad" to you, isn't a happy thought. But let's talk about having a "strange man" in the house.

You may not meet all the men your mom goes out with. There may be a few she dates once and won't date again. But if she meets someone she likes really well, she'll see more of him. And at that point, when she's seeing more of him, she'll certainly introduce him to you.

You'll probably begin doing some things together. She may invite him to have dinner with you and her. He may even invite you and your mom to his house, with him cooking dinner. He may take you and your mom to the movies or miniature golf or some other fun place. You'll get used to having him around.

At some point, your mom might decide he's really the right man for her. Then she and he might talk about getting married. But by the time they do get married, and he moves in with your mom and you, he won't be a "strange man" anymore. You'll know him. You'll have spent time with him. You'll start getting comfortable around him.

It might still feel funny, at first, to have him living there. He isn't your dad. No matter how close you get to your mom's new husband, he won't take your dad's place. And he's not trying to replace him.

But what's wrong with having both a dad and a stepdad? What are some of the things you like to do with your dad? Think of them all. But you don't get to do them as much, now that your dad doesn't live with you, do you?

If your mom does get married again, you wouldn't have to call her new husband "Dad." You've got a dad already. And any man your mom marries will understand that.

➤ *What would I call Mom's new husband?*

He might let you call him by his first name. You might be comfortable calling him "Pop" or some other fatherly name that isn't "Dad." Or he may have a nickname you can call him by. You might even think of a name you want to call him that's your own special name for him.

Suppose your mom gets married again. You'd have your dad to do all those favorite things with whenever you're with him . . . and your stepdad to do them with the rest of the time. That's not such a bad deal, is it? It actually sounds pretty good! (If it's still hard to think about right now, don't worry — it may be a long time, if ever, before you're in this situation. And by the time you have to deal with it, it will be easier for you.)

➤ *What if Dad remarries?*

Now, we've talked about how things might be when your mom starts dating and if she gets married again; but the same things will be true for your dad if he dates and remarries. A stepmom won't ever replace your mom, but she can be someone who cares about you and is fun to be with.

Here are some important things to remember when your parents start dating new people:

• Your mom is not being disloyal if she dates other men. She is not married to your dad anymore. Your dad is not being disloyal to date other women, either.

• Even if your mom gets remarried, your dad is still your dad.

• And if your dad remarries, your mom is still your mom.

• You do not have to call your mom's new husband "Dad" (unless you want to). You do not have to call your dad's new wife "Mom," unless you want to, either.

• You can like your mom's new husband — or even love him — without being disloyal to your dad. The same is true about your dad's new wife.

Whether your parents start dating again or not, no matter what happens, remember that you will *always* be their child and will *always* hold a special place in each of their hearts.

10

Important Stuff
to Remember

Here's a short list of some of the most important stuff I hope you got out of this book:

• **The divorce is not your fault.** It is not because you did anything wrong. Even if Dad and Mom seem more annoyed at you than usual lately, *that does not mean the divorce was in any way your fault*. They are annoyed easily because they are going through a tough time.

• **It's OK to miss the parent who has moved out.** It's OK even if the parent you're living with doesn't miss the parent who's gone.

• **You do not have to lose touch with the parent who moved out.** If he (or she) stays nearby, you will have regular visiting times with him or her.

• **You don't have to lose touch even if your parent moves out of town, or you and the parent you live with move out of town.** You will get visiting vacations. And there are lots of ways to keep in touch in between visits.

• **It's OK to feel sad or angry.** Try to find good ways to work with your feelings. Don't hurt other people just because you're hurting.

• **It's OK to cry. (And it's OK *not* to cry.)** There are lots of ways to help yourself to feel better, though. If an old toy or outgrown piece of clothing makes you feel better, it's OK to use it to help yourself.

• **It's OK to feel angry at your parents for getting divorced.** But remember, they're getting divorced because they think it's the best thing to do. They are not doing it easily, or on a whim. They are not doing it to hurt you.

• **Your house may be a nicer place to live now,** if your mom and dad were fighting before. Once they're not living together anymore, the day-to-day fighting will stop.

• **Even if you didn't hear them fighting, they were unhappy with each other.** Otherwise, they wouldn't be getting divorced. After they're divorced, things should be a little less stressful for both of them. They may both be more relaxed and happier. And that will make things more pleasant for you.

• **You do not have to choose sides.** The divorce is between them. You are not being asked who was right, or which parent you love more. This is strictly a grown-up matter, between your parents.

• **If your parents have seemed unhappy with you lately, it's just because of the tensions they're feeling. *It's not you.***

• **They are both still your parents,** even though they don't live together anymore. They both still love you. You still have a family.

• **When you go to visit your dad (or mom) in his (or her) new home, it's going to feel strange in the beginning.** Give it time. It will feel less strange as time goes by.

• **Your parents are human.** They make mistakes too — nobody's perfect. If they ask you to carry messages to each other, or spy on each other, you can say "No." You *should* say "No," if it doesn't feel right to you.

• **It's OK to like other people your parents start dating.**

• **Your mom or dad might someday marry someone else.** You don't have to call Dad's new wife

"Mom." You don't have to call Mom's new husband "Dad." You already have a mom and a dad. And these people will respect that.

• **Most important of all:** *Parents who love you will not stop loving you.* Even if your mom and dad have stopped loving each other, the love parents have for their kids is different and special.

Bill of Rights for Children Whose Parents Are Divorced

Children have the right to:

- Know the truth about the divorce, with simple explanations!

- Be protected from the parental warfare!

- Develop and maintain an independent relationship with each parent!

- Be free from having to take sides with, defend, or denigrate either parent!

- Be free of responsibility for having caused the divorce!

- Be reassured that they are not to blame!

- Be free from having to take over parental responsibilities! A child can't become the "man of the house" or the "little mother"!

- Expect that both parents will follow through with the parenting plan and honor specific commitments for scheduled time with their child!

- Expect that both parents will inform each other about medical, dental, education and legal matters concerning the child!

- Receive love, guidance, patience, understanding, and limits from their parents!

- Spend time with each parent, regardless of financial support!

- Be financially supported by both parents, regardless of how much time is spent with either parent!

- Maintain privacy when talking to either parent on the telephone!

- Have a personal sleeping area and space for possessions in each parent's home!

- Participate in age-appropriate activities so long as those activities do not significantly impair their relationship with either parent!

- Avoid being told the painful details of their parents' legal proceedings!

- Avoid being made to feel guilty for loving both parents!

- Avoid making the custody/visitation decisions!

- Avoid being cross-examined by one parent after spending time with the other parent!

- Not to be used as a messenger or spy between the parents!

- Not to be asked to keep secrets from the other parent.

From *Parenting After Divorce: A Guide to Resolving Conflicts and Meeting Your Children's Needs* © 2000 by Philip M. Stahl, Ph.D. Reproduced by permission of Impact Publishers, Inc.

Note to Parents

Hugh R. Leavell, Ph.D., P.A.

Divorce. It's a choice made by adults to dissolve a marriage that doesn't work anymore. It will be painful, stressful and sad. It will include feelings of anger and grief over past insults and present losses as well as fear for the future. It's likely, also, to involve some feelings of relief for the couple. For one or both of them, the decision reflects a desire for change, to right a wrong, to make new choices about living that are more appropriate to current circumstances. Because they're adults they have resources they can bring to bear, both for coping with and for understanding the changes they're living through. After all, they are the ones creating the situation.

For the kids it's different. They never asked for or expected this. The only world they've ever known, the safe, familiar place where life began, is coming apart around them. They have no control over it. They don't understand the whys and wherefores. And it wouldn't help if they did. That wouldn't put what's been shattered back together again. Suddenly, the very fabric of love upon which confidence, trust, identity and self-worth have been faithfully stitched is being torn to threads. They will wish they could patch it back together somehow, that Mom and Dad would turn to each other again and try to love one more time, for the family, for us, because we don't want to lose what we have, because we don't want to change, not that way.

Kids don't understand what reality and time can do to love between adults. They don't know about the pressures of the world, about how love can change and go away, about how we can survive this loss and others. Theirs is a pre-Copernican universe in which the self seems to be the center of everything. Only gradually will knowledge and maturity bring an awareness of how things really are, of how love can die in one relationship and continue to bloom in another, of how families can exist and take care of each other even after they've changed shape, of the permanent and immutable love a parent feels for his or her child, no matter what.

What kids need is reassurance. The world isn't ending but it may feel like it is. The stakes are higher for them because they feel as though their very lives depend on the love their parents feel for them. They know they need to be taken care of by someone who understands their needs and loves them very much. And, if love can end between him and her, the god and goddess of the home, the givers of life itself, then, might it not also end between him or her and me? Where would I be then? Would I survive? Who would care for me then? For kids, this is a life and death issue, at least in their fantasies.

Everyone knows about kids and their fantasies. Not grounded as adults are in the everyday practice of necessary reality, kids can get carried away with their fantasies. The monster that lives in the closet, the old dead tree that becomes a ghost in the night, the vague, shapeless, nameless fears that accompany sadness and stress, these are just a few examples of typical childish fantasies.

When kids worry, they sometimes don't know when to quit. And kids do worry, plenty. They need an adult to tell them what's what, how to hold onto themselves, what's real and what's not, what's OK and what's not, what to expect and how to handle it when it happens. That's what Cynthia MacGregor does for kids in *The Divorce Helpbook for Kids.*

Cynthia's is the voice of a wise, older person, explaining cataclysmic life changes in a way that is reassuring without condescension. She doesn't minimize the magnitude and variety of changes children face when their parents break up but she doesn't "hystericize" them either. Hers is a calming voice, but an engaging and lively one, too. She acknowledges the pain and confusion and frustration inherent in a child's journey through his or her parents' divorce, but she doesn't encourage hopeless, helpless wallowing. Instead, she gets right down to practical matters, explaining some of the basic technical issues of divorce, offering enough information but not too much. And, always, she makes the issues breathe and pulse with life by taking us into the lives and minds of particular children who are struggling to cope with those same issues in their lives.

This is not just a book for kids about divorce, though. It's a book about life after divorce, too. The kids in Cynthia's book are dealing with visitation and custody and straddling two households and making it all work. Maybe it isn't easy but it is possible and it is necessary. And these are the real issues kids face. "Why do I have different bedtimes in Mom's house and Dad's house?" "What if Mom and Dad try to communicate through me?" "How should I feel about new people in Mom's and Dad's lives?" "Who's to blame for all this mayhem, anyway?" (No one, thank you.) This is practical help for real kids with real parents living real lives in the real world.

Kids with divorced parents, living in single-parent families or with stepparents or blended families used to be a minority. They felt like misfits in a world of intact, nuclear families composed of Mom, Dad and their biological offspring. Things have changed. Now it's normal to have parents who are divorced. But that doesn't mean it's easy. It's still hard to go through the changes and the loss and the fear and sadness when a family breaks up. It still threatens a child's basic security and trust in love and in the stability of family. We know now that some of these effects are profound and permanent, contributing in a major way to that child's personality and outlook on life, love, family and self. Yet, perhaps, the effect is no worse than that of living with a loveless, depressed marriage or, worse still, a violent, abusive one. In any case, as long as there is marriage there will be divorce, and as long as there is divorce there will be children of divorce. These kids need some help. Here's a little "helpbook," written in a way kids will enjoy and understand, to guide them through separation, divorce and life after divorce.

Glossary
What All Those Big Words Mean

abuse: to hurt (a person) by treating badly, or to misuse (a thing). Hitting a child is an example of *child abuse*. Hitting a wife or husband is an example of *spousal abuse*. Taking drugs or alcohol to get high is an example of *substance abuse*. Attacking another person with harsh or unkind words is an example of *verbal abuse*.

alimony: money — like an allowance — that a court orders to be paid to one spouse (wife or husband) by the other spouse after a legal separation or divorce.

attorney/lawyer: a person who is trained in law, and has the legal power to advise or act for another person in legal matters.

boundaries: the lines or limits between two things, such as the property line between you and your neighbor, or the "line" where your space ends and another person's space begins.

brainstorming: trying to come up with as many different ideas as you can.

career: a work life, or a series of jobs. Your parent may have a *career* as a teacher, or a mechanic, or a fireman, or a secretary, or . . .

child support: money that the court orders to be paid by one parent to the other to help take care of the child(ren). Usually the money must be paid every month.

chores: small jobs you may have at home, such as doing dishes, taking out trash, mowing the lawn.

clergyperson: a religious leader, such as a pastor, minister, priest, rabbi.

complaint: something a person is upset about. A gripe. In courts, a *complaint* is the name of the paper one person gives to the judge that tells about his or her problems with the other person. (see also *criticism*)

confide: to tell someone in secret. To "confide in" a friend, or counselor, or parent means to tell that person things that are important to you, things that you don't want others to know about.

counselor: a person who is trained to help others when they're having problems. Your school counselor can help you learn to deal with playground bullies, or to get rid of your fear of speaking up in class, or to feel better when things aren't going well in your life.

court: the people (judges, for instance) who manage the laws, and the building where they meet to do their work. The *divorce court* means the judge and the building where divorces are ordered.

criticism: finding something wrong with a person or a thing. Some people show a lot of *criticism* of other people's looks, or actions, or ideas. (see also *complaint*)

criticizing: giving criticism to another person or thing.

crime: an action that is against the law. Robbing a bank or stealing a car is a *crime*.

custodial parent: the parent with whom a child lives, and the one who is mostly in charge of the child's life.

custody: to be in charge of someone or something. The parent you live with most of the time has *custody* of you. (see also *joint custody*)

custody evaluator: the person who figures out a child's best interests and recommends a parenting plan to the judge. For instance, the *custody evaluator* may tell the judge that the child should spend half of the time with each parent after the divorce. This person may also be called a *custody investigator* or *custody assessor.*

deposition: a statement given by a witness before a trial. Think of giving a report in class, and meeting with the teacher before your report to tell her what you're going to say in the report. What you tell her in that meeting before your report is like a *deposition.* Of course, in a real legal deposition, the questions are usually asked by an attorney (not a teacher!) who wants to find out what the person (probably not you!) will say in court. (see also *testimony*)

disagreement: when two people don't have the same ideas about something, they disagree, and a *disagreement* happens. Some disagreements aren't important, but some are very serious, and can lead to fights between friends or neighbors, divorces between married people, or even wars between countries,

disloyal: when someone is not true to someone else. Telling stories behind someone's back, lying about someone, cheating someone, and playing favorites can be *disloyal*.

dispute: a *dispute* is about the same thing as a *disagreement*, but it usually means that the disagreement will be settled in a court.

divorce: the legal ending of a marriage. *Divorce* happens when the court says the marriage is officially over.

divorce decree: the legal papers from the court that tell everyone when and how the divorce officially ends.

divorce mediation: helping a married couple to work out the plan for their divorce before they go to court for the official papers. Usually a trained person called a *mediator* works with the couple to help them figure out how to handle child custody, money, the house, the cars, and other important things in their lives as they break up their marriage.

e-mail: messages sent from one person to another on computers hooked up to telephone lines.

800 number: a phone number that allows person #1 to call person #2, and have person #2 pay for the call. You can call someone who has an 800 number and it won't cost you anything. The person or business that you call has to pay. (Also true with "888" or "877" numbers.)

emotions: feelings, such as anger, fear, rage, sadness.

equal: things or people are "equal" when they have the same rights, privileges, or values. When parents have equal rights in raising their children, they both have a say in all decisions, so they should agree on such things as money, school, values, religion, rules, and so on (or else they have to figure out a way to settle their disagreement!).

familiar: people or things that are well-known to you, comfortable, easy to be with. They've been around you for a while.

family court: a court for family law cases, where divorces, custody, and other family problems are settled.

fantasy: a dream, or a daydream, or a picture in your mind of how things might be. Fantasies can be historic (castles and knights and dragons), or futuristic (spaceships and planets), or present time (your parents getting back together). Fantasies are only in your imagination; they're not real.

guilty: being wrong, doing a crime. In court, guilty means the court has ruled that the person has done something against the law.

hearing: a meeting of the people involved (for example, the parents and their attorneys) with a judge before there is a trial. Sometimes things can be worked out at a *hearing* so there doesn't have to be a trial. Both a hearing and a trial give everybody a chance to be heard by a *judge* or *mediator* or *special master*.

impolite: not polite, not courteous, not being nice to others.

information: facts, knowledge, data. When you have *information* about something or someone, it means you know about what has happened with that thing or person. Of course, your information could be wrong!

innocent: not guilty, being right, not doing a crime. In court, *innocent* means the court has ruled that the person has not done a crime.

interrogate: to ask lots of questions.

jealousy: a feeling of envy that another person might take your place. Children are sometimes *jealous* of step-brothers and sisters who have time with their parent. Moms (and dads) are sometimes jealous of new people that dads (and moms) may be dating.

joint custody: a parenting plan that gives each parent a lot of time with the child. Sometimes people say *joint custody* when they mean 50-50, but it doesn't have to mean equal time. *Shared custody* is also used as a name for joint custody.

journal: a diary or private book of notes to keep track of your feelings and what's happening in your life.

judge: the person who's in charge at the court, and who — in family court cases — makes the decisions about divorces, custody, parenting plans. You've probably seen actors on TV who play judges and wear black robes. Real judges wear black robes too, but they aren't playing.

lawyer: (see *attorney/lawyer*)

legal: actions that follow the law or the rules. If you do what the laws require, your behavior will be *legal*, and you won't get in trouble.

legal custody: a parent's right to make decisions for a child about education, religious training, health care, money, and other matters. If *legal custody* is also *joint custody*, the parents share these decisions.

loneliness: a sad feeling when you are alone, sometimes if you think you have no friends, or no one to talk with.

mediation: (see *divorce mediation*)

mediator: a trained person who works with a couple to help them figure out how to handle decisions about custody, money, and other matters they may have trouble agreeing upon.

messages: thoughts, ideas, suggestions, questions, orders that are passed from one person to another, usually in writing. It's best if moms and dads give *messages* directly to each other, and not ask their children to carry them.

motherly figure: a woman who can act or seem like a kind of mother when your real mother is not around. Sometimes a grandmother or step-mother or aunt can be a *motherly figure*.

non-custodial parent: the parent you don't live with after the divorce.

online service: a company that helps you connect to the Internet or the World Wide Web on a computer.

out of place: a feeling of being uncomfortable, not at home, strange, uneasy.

paralegal: a person who works for an attorney, and is trained to find out all about the laws and help the attorney get ready for a hearing or trial.

parent education: a special program set up by the court that helps parents understand their own feelings about divorce and helps them work out a plan for shared custody of the children after a divorce.

parental alienation: when one parent tries to make the child(ren) not like the other parent any more. *Parental alienation* is a very sad thing that doesn't happen very often, but it can happen when the parents are *really, really* angry at each other, and don't like or trust each other at all.

parenting plan: a plan that tells how the parents will share custody and visitation. Most *parenting plans* tell about how the parents want to raise the children, what the schedules will be for school and holidays and vacations, who will pay for school and clothes and housing and other expenses, how transportation will be worked out, and how disagreements will be settled. *Parenting plans* are not used everywhere, however.

permanent custody award: the final decision of the court that says how the parents will share custody of the child(ren) in a divorce. Everybody has to live by the *permanent custody* decision unless the court changes it in the future. The main thing the court decides about is the long-term best interests of the child for a good home, a loving parent, and a secure future.

primary custodial parent: the parent that the child spends most of the time with. In *shared custody* or *joint custody* plans, neither parent is the *primary custodial parent*.

primary nurturing parent: the parent who does the most to take care of the child's needs for love and care is called the *primary nurturing parent*. In many families, of course, both parents share the job of providing love and care, even after a divorce.

privileges: rights, things you are allowed to do.

professionals: people who are experts, who are paid to do certain jobs — often those who help others, such as doctors, lawyers, accountants, psychologists, therapists.

property settlement: the plan to divide up the money, house, car(s), furniture, and other things a couple owns. The *property settlement* is ordered by the court in a divorce. Often the couple works out a plan on their own, and the court approves it.

psychological evaluation: several things done by a psychologist to find out more about the people involved in a divorce (the children or the parents or both). The evaluation may include conversations, tests, home visits, or other methods.

psychologist: a special doctor who is an expert in knowing about people's thoughts and feelings and actions. Sometimes *psychologists* help adults and children understand and handle their feelings. *Psychologists* also can help people learn how to get along better.

realistic: down to earth; something that is from the real world; solid ideas that are useful in everyday life.

referee: a person appointed by the court to help make decisions in a divorce or custody case. Kind of like a soccer or football *referee*, except this referee's decisions affect people's lives for a long time, so they must be approved by the court. Sometimes a *referee* is called a *special master* or *parent coordinator*.

relatives: members of a family, such as mother, father, brother, sister, grandparents, aunts, uncles, cousins . . . Relatives may be related directly (by "blood") or indirectly (by marriage).

responsibility: a job to do. Taking *responsibility* is doing your share of what needs to be done, doing what is right, doing what is required of you, keeping promises.

roommate: a person who lives with someone else, sharing a living space (house or apartment or dormitory room). Roommates don't need to be related; they just live in the same place. Husbands and wives are not usually called *roommates*, even though they live together.

routine: regular habits, or steps, or ways to do things. Getting up in the morning, having breakfast, brushing your teeth, and going to school make up a kind of "routine."

separation: parents living apart, but not yet legally divorced. (see also *trial separation*)

shared physical custody: the child spends some time with each parent. It may or may not be an equal sharing of time. (see also *joint custody* and *shared custody*)

shared custody: (see also *joint custody* and *shared physical custody*)

situation: what's happening in somebody's life. Having the bases loaded with two out in the bottom of the ninth is a tough *situation*. So is having the scenery collapse in the middle of the school play, or having your music stand fall over just before your big solo. Having your dog come home after he was gone for hours is a nice situation; so is being chosen to lead your 4-H group into the arena at the county fair.

special master: (see *referee*)

stressful: tense, hurtful, painful, hard to handle, something that makes your heart race or makes you feel nervous. (see also *tension*)

supervised exchanges: turning a child over from one parent to the other when there is another person present to supervise. This is sometimes done when the parents are very angry at each other and need help with the exchange.

supervised visitation: when the court orders *supervised visitation*, the non-custodial parent may have visits with the child only when another person is with them for the visit. The other person may be a relative or friend, or someone who is paid to help protect the child.

temporary child support: short-term support for a child that is ordered by the court until the final decisions (see *divorce decree*) are made by the judge.

temporary custody award: the temporary decision of the court that says how the parents will share custody of the child(ren) in a divorce. Everybody has to live by the *temporary custody* decision until the court makes its *permanent custody* decision in the future. The decisions may be different. That is, the child(ren) may be ordered to live with one parent temporarily, and the other parent permanently. It depends on what the court thinks is best for the child(ren).

tension: nervousness, stress, discomfort because of a problem that's going on. Sometimes you'll feel butterflies in your stomach, muscle tightness, faster heartbeat, cold hands. Some children feel this way before a test or oral report in school; others feel it lots of the time during a divorce. (see also *stressful*)

testify: to answer questions in court. The questions are usually asked by attorneys, or could be asked by the judge. Parents who don't have attorneys will ask questions themselves.

testimony: what a witness says to the court. (see also *testify* and *witness*)

therapist: a professional who is trained to help people solve problems. Some therapists are also psychologists, others are marriage and family therapists, and some are experts in helping children. (see also *counselor* and *psychologist*)

trial: a court meeting where the judge, the attorneys, the witnesses, and the people involved (usually the parents in a divorce or custody trial), work out a decision about what the law says will happen to the people involved. In a custody trial, for example, everyone will have a say, and the judge will decide how the parents will divide up custody of the child(ren).

trial separation: a time for parents to live apart to see if they can work out their problems.

visitation: time children spend with the parent they don't live with. The court may order a specific schedule for visitation, such as "Tuesday nights and every other weekend." (see also *non-custodial parent*)

visitation rights: the rights of the non-custodial parent to spend time with the children who don't live with him (or her).

witness: someone who saw what happened. In a trial, a *witness* will tell the court what he or she saw.

This list of "What All Those Big Words Mean" was prepared by Robert E. Alberti, Ph.D. (Impact Publishers, Inc.), in consultation with psychologist Pat Palmer, Ed.D. (Maui, Hawaii), psychologist Philip M. Stahl, Ph.D. (Dublin, California), Judge (Ret.) James Stewart (San Jose, California), attorney Barbara Walton, Esq. (Meadville, Pennsylvania), and the author.

Resources for Parents and Children

Books for Parents

Ackerman, M. *"Does Wednesday Mean Mom's House or Dad's?"*: *Parenting Together While Living Apart* (2nd Edition). New York: John Wiley & Sons, 2008.

Berry, D. *The Divorce Recovery Sourcebook.* New York: McGraw-Hill, 1998.

Beyer, R. & Winchester, K. *Speaking of Divorce: How to Talk with Your Kids and Help Them Cope.* Minneapolis, MN: Free Spirit Publishing, 2001.

Einstein, E. & Albert, L. *Strengthening Your Stepfamily.* Atascadero, CA: Impact Publishers, 2006.

Everett, C. & Everett, S.V. *The Healthy Divorce.* San Francisco, CA: Jossey-Bass, 1998.

Fisher, B. & Alberti, R. *Rebuilding: When Your Relationship Ends* (3rd Edition). Atascadero, CA: Impact Publishers, 2006.

Kranitz, M.A. *Getting Apart Together: The Couple's Guide to a Fair Divorce or Separation* (2nd Edition). Atascadero, CA: Impact Publishers, 2000.

Krantzler, M. *The Creative Divorce.* New York: eReads.com, 2002.

Lyster, M. *Building a Parenting Agreement That Works* (6th Edition). Berkeley, CA: Nolo Press, 2007.

MacGregor, C. *Jigsaw Puzzle Family: The Stepkids' Guide to Fitting It Together.* Atascadero, CA: Impact Publishers, 2005.

MacGregor, C. & Alberti, R. *After Your Divorce: Creating the Good Life on Your Own.* Atascadero, CA: Impact Publishers, 2006.

Mason, M.A. *The Custody Wars: Why Children Are Losing the Legal Battle and What We Can Do About It.* New York: Basic Books, 1999.

Neuman, M.G. *Helping Your Kids Cope with Divorce the Sandcastles Way.* New York: Random House, 1999.

Ricci, I. *Mom's House, Dad's House: A Complete Guide for Parents Who Are Separated, Divorced, or Remarried* (2nd Edition). New York: Fireside, 1997.

Stahl, P.M. *Parenting After Divorce: Resolving Conflicts and Meeting Your Children's Needs* (2nd Edition). Atascadero, CA: Impact Publishers, 2007.

Stewart, J.W. *The Child Custody Book: How to Protect Your Children and Win Your Case.* Atascadero, CA: Impact Publishers, 2000.

Talia, M.S. *How to Avoid the Divorce From Hell — and Dance Together at Your Daughter's Wedding* (2nd Edition). San Ramon, CA: Nexus Publishing Company, 2006.

Temlock, M. *Your Child's Divorce: What to Expect — What You Can Do.* Atascadero, CA: Impact Publishers, 2006.

Walton, B. *101 Little Instructions for Surviving Your Divorce: A No-Nonsense Guide to the Challenges at Hand.* Atascadero, CA: Impact Publishers, 1999.

Webb, D. *50 Ways to Love Your Leaver: Getting on With Your Life After the Breakup*. Atascadero, CA: Impact Publishers, 2000.

Books for Children

(Ages 4-8)

Brown, L.K. and Brown, M. *Dinosaurs Divorce: A Guide for Changing Families*. Boston: Little, Brown & Company, 1988.

Lansky, V. *It's Not Your Fault, Koko Bear: A Read-Together Book for Parents & Young Children During Divorce*. Minnetonka, MN: Book Peddlers, 1998.

Nightingale, L. *My Parents Still Love Me*. Yorba Linda, CA: Nightingale Rose Publications, 1997.

Palmer, P. *"I wish I could hold your hand . . .": A Child's Guide to Grief and Loss*. Atascadero, CA: Impact Publishers, 2000.

Ransom, J.E. *I Don't Want to Talk About It*. Washington, D.C.: Magination Press, 2000.

Stinson, K. *Mom and Dad Don't Live Together Anymore* (Revised Edition). Vancouver, Canada: Annick Press, 2007.

(Ages 7-12)

Beyer, R. & Winchester, K. *What in the World Do You Do When Your Parents Divorce?* Minneapolis, MN: Free Spirit Publishing, 2001.

Williams, M. *Cool Cats, Calm Kids: Relaxation & Stress Management for Young People*. Atascadero, CA: Impact Publishers, 2005.

(Ages 9 and up)

Blackstone-Ford, J., et al. *My Parents Are Divorced, Too: A Book for Kids by Kids* (2nd Edition). Washington, D.C.: Magination Press, 2006.

Blume, J. *It's Not the End of the World* (Revised Edition). Scarsdale, New York: Atheneum, 2002.

MacGregor, C. *The Divorce Helpbook for Teens.* Atascadero, CA: Impact Publishers, 2004.

Pickhardt, C. *The Case of the Scary Divorce.* Washington, D.C: Magination Press, 1997.

Ricci, I. *Mom's House, Dad's House for Kids: Feeling at Home in One Home or Two.* New York: Fireside, 2006.

Stern, E.S., et al. *Divorce Is Not the End of the World: Zoe's and Evan's Coping Guide for Kids* (Revised Edition). Berkeley, CA: Tricycle Press, 2008.

(All Ages)

Johnston, J., Editor. *Through the Eyes of Children: Healing Stories for Children of Divorce.* New York: Free Press, 1997.

Krementz, J. *How It Feels When Parents Divorce.* New York: Knopf, 1988.

Web Resources

www.womansdivorce.com

www.divorcemagazine.com

www.kidsturn.org

www.4children.org

www.divorcesource.com

www.kidsturncentral.com/topics/issues/divorce.htm

www.helpguide.org/mental/children_divorce.htm

www.kidshealth.org/kid/feeling/home_family/divorce.html

www.mayoclinic.com/health/divorce/HO00055

Index

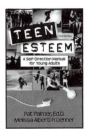

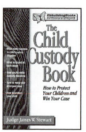